Your Three- and Four-Year-Old

As They Grow

Your Three- and Four-Year-Old

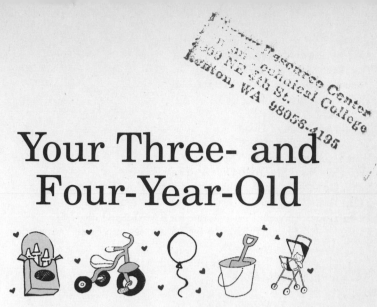

As They Grow

By the Editors of **Parents** Magazine
and Ginny Graves

St. Martin's Griffin ≋ New York

Also by Parents Magazine:
The Parents Answer Book
Parents Magazine's It Worked for Me!
The Parents Party Book
Play and Learn
The Parents Book of Lists
Your One-Year-Old: As They Grow
Your Two-Year-Old: As They Grow
Your Five- and Six-Year-Old: As They Grow
I Can Do It!: Physical Milestones for the First Twelve Months
I Can Do It!: Physical Milestones for One-Year-Olds
I Can Do It!: Physical Milestones for Two-Year-Olds
I Can Do It!: Physical Milestones for Three- and Four-Year-Olds

A Roundtable Press Book

For Roundtable Press, Inc.:
Directors: Julie Merberg, Marsha Melnick, Susan E. Meyer
Project editor: Meredith Wolf Schizer
Designer: Laura Smyth
Computer production: Carrie Glidden
Illustrator: Penny Carter

For Parents Magazine:
Editor in chief: Sally Lee
Deputy editor: Linda Fears
G+J Director of Books and Licensing: Tammy Palazzo

www.stmartins.com

ISBN 0-312-26420-8

First St. Martin's Griffin Edition: November 2000

10 9 8 7 6 5 4 3 2 1

Contents

I'm the best! 100
Your three- to four-year-old's personality

Trucks and tea sets 112
Your three- to four-year-old's gender identity

But I don't want to! 127
Your three- to four-year-old's behavior

Foreword

by Sally Lee

Making friends, expressing emotions, riding a trike, dressing all by herself. . . . These are just a few of the amazing milestones your child will experience during her preschool years—a truly exciting, joyful time in both your lives. She'll regularly remind you that she's a "big kid" now—and you'll notice dramatic physical changes as your child loses baby fat and becomes taller, leaner, and more muscular. Emotionally, your child will become much more attuned to other people's feelings, begin to learn how to cooperate and negotiate, and start to build up self-esteem and a feeling of competence.

This book is the perfect guide for parents to help their three- and four-year-olds negotiate all the new changes in their lives. We'll explain the complex world of imaginary playmates, help you understand the whims of a picky eater, teach you how to calm his newfound fears, and perhaps most importantly, help you get him ready for his first real school experience.

I want to do it myself!

Your three- to four-year-old's growing independence

Maybe it will hit you when you see your child from afar frolicking on the playground, or when you carry her to bed one night and can hardly lift her, or when you're packing up yet another box of her outgrown clothes: Your baby is no longer a baby—or even a toddler. She has become a miniature person in a way she's never been before. She's taller and leaner (even her face looks longer!), with less baby fat padding her gangly limbs. She can talk a blue streak—and does. For the first time, she can really describe what she's thinking and feeling, and her near-constant commentary on the world around her is likely to leave you amused and bemused in equal measure.

Emotionally, your child is growing up, too. The egocentricity of a two-year-old is starting, slowly, to give way to a more externally focused, empathetic perspective. As a result, your child is beginning to see you as a distinct person, with needs, feelings, and a point of view separate from her own. Prepare yourself. When your child makes the intellectual leap from "Mommy and Daddy are an extension of me" to "Mommy and Daddy are unique individuals," she may be as moody and unpredictable as an adolescent.

On the one hand, there will be days (hopefully lots of them) when she'll be cooperative and eager to please. At this age, she identifies with you and yearns for your approval. On the other hand, she'll have moments when she's extremely willful, which may get worse before it starts to improve around age five. (You may even find yourself pining for the Terrible Twos once your child reaches the Frightful Fours!) To a young child, often the quickest path to independence is through aggression and defiance, so don't be surprised when your preschooler runs away when you tell her it's time to get dressed, or refuses to budge when you ask her to go for a walk. Her behavior is her way of letting you know she's an individual with her own agenda.

Likewise, it's not unusual for a four-year-old to believe she knows more than her parents. She may regularly test the limits of your power in an effort to stake out her own unique claim on the universe. Routines like getting dressed, going to bed, and eating meals may turn into mini battlegrounds for a while, until your child eventually, by the end of her fourth year, gets more comfortable with her place in the scheme of things.

Physically, your child's stratospheric learning curve will slow just slightly in the coming years, but she'll continue to add new skills and spend lots of time polishing her old ones. Indeed, the deftness with which she does things is probably the single most striking aspect of this age. The skills she performed somewhat clumsily at age two—feeding herself, stacking blocks, running, and jumping—she now handles with amazing finesse. The control your child has gained over her body makes her eager to tackle increasingly difficult tasks and to prove that she's a "big kid." While it may be easy to applaud her efforts at jumping on one foot or swinging hand-over-hand on the monkey bars, you're likely to cringe at some of her endeavors, like when she insists on clearing her own dinner plate from the table (and shatters the plate when it falls to the floor) or tries to climb a tree. Still, such accomplishments will give her a sense of pride, and allowing her to push the limits of her physical ability (within reason, of course) will give her a solid base of self-confidence and competence that will serve her well in the coming years.

Be warned, however. Although your three-year-old may bowl you over with her physical prowess, she still needs lots of guidance, support, and encouragement. Critical aspects of real maturity, like judgment and self-control, are still lacking at this age, and you'll see proof of it frequently, like when, heedless of oncoming traffic, she darts after a ball that rolls into the street, or when she throws a fit because she wants to go to the park *right now,* not one hour from now. Figuring out how to back off and let your child explore her independence, but still be there for her when she needs you, will be one of your biggest challenges during the next two years.

The ages of three and four are a time of transition, when your protected, sheltered baby is preparing to make a daring leap into the wider world of school. To aid her metamorphosis into a true individual, this is a good time to enroll your child in preschool. *(See pages 50–51 for details on how to choose a good one.)* This can give her a taste of what school is like in a low-key, play-focused environment and get her used to the idea of being away from you for a portion of the day, if she hasn't already done so.

As preschoolers venture farther out into the wide world, they will still come running back for regular reassurance from parents

i want to do it myself! 11

and caregivers. This swinging back and forth between independence and dependence, bravery and fearfulness is perfectly normal. Your child needs to practice letting go so she's able to do it when the time comes, but she also needs your stable, predictable, loving presence in order to feel safe. Although the move away from parents is unmistakable at this age, in ways your child needs you more than ever—to teach her about safety and right and wrong, and create a secure environment with consistent rules and limits as she prepares for life as a school-age child.

DEVELOPMENTAL MILESTONE
Caring for oneself

These are heady days for your three- to four-year-old. Mere months ago, she was an uncoordinated, tumble-prone toddler. Now, she not only walks with ease, she can run, climb, hop, skip, ride a tricycle, and probably even throw and catch a ball. Many of the things she's seen older children and adults do she can now do herself, and the feeling of independence this gives her is likely to fill her with pride.

No wonder she runs ahead of you every time you're out for a walk or demands, "I want to do it myself!" when you try to help her put on her pajamas. She's understandably eager to show off, and perfect, her newfound skills. After years of relying on someone else for help, imagine the thrill of being able to put on your own pants for the first time, or brush your teeth, or eat a bowl of cereal without spilling most of it on your shirt. Having only recently reached those hard-won physical milestones, your child isn't likely to want to relinquish control anytime soon. Here are some of the things she's probably able to do now, or will be able to do soon:

Dress and undress herself, at least partially. Most children this age won't be able to tie their own shoes or fasten small buttons, but they can work zippers (if you get them started), snaps, and sometimes large buttons.

Go to the bathroom. The normal range of toilet teaching is 24 to 36 months, although children may learn somewhat earlier or later. Newly taught children may need help with wiping (some even need assistance until age five or six) and may need to be reminded to go, especially when they're involved in a fun game or activity.

Handle a spoon and fork with ease. She probably still will need you to cut her food, though. Unless your child is dressed in an outfit that needs to be dry-cleaned, you can put away those soiled baby bibs (finally!).

Drink from a regular cup. Also, she usually will be able to pour juice or milk from a lightweight container without spilling.

Brush her teeth. She may do slipshod work, though. To be sure her teeth are truly clean, do a speedy brush after she has finished.

Pedal a tricycle. Most children accomplish this feat between the ages of 30 and 48 months, thanks to their increased coordination and strength.

Grasp a crayon, pencil, or paintbrush with three fingers and thumb to color, draw, and paint with greater precision. Your child's artwork will evolve over the course of these two years, and human figures will begin emerging from her scribbles. By the end of the preschool stage, your child should even have the muscular coordination and concentration to be able to print some letters and, most likely, her name.

Use scissors. Just be sure that they have rounded edges, or, if they don't, that her cutting is supervised.

Throw, catch, and kick a ball.

SAFETY FIRST
Safeguarding your preschooler

As your child becomes more capable of playing by herself, it might feel like you no longer have to worry so much about her safety. Unfortunately, that's not true. While household safety remains a priority, your focus needs to expand to include the outdoors, where your child will spend increasing amounts of time. Although preschoolers are starting to grasp certain key notions of safety, like cause and effect, they lack the tools to police their own behavior. Even many four-year-olds still believe that their wishes and expectations actually control what happens, a "magical" thought process that can get them into a lot of trouble. For instance, although your preschooler may know that cars are dangerous, she might run in front of one anyway, believing that the car will stop simply because she wants it to.

That doesn't mean you should shelter your child or insist she stay in view every minute of the day. But you do need to understand the hazards—and take precautionary measures to protect her.

Around the house. As long as her room is fully childproofed—with electrical outlets covered and all breakable objects removed—you can let your child play alone for as long as she's willing. It's a good idea to check on her every ten minutes or so, but giving your child some space will allow her to immerse herself in the imaginary play that is so critical at this age and discover the joy of her own company.

In the car. Because of the explosive power of air bags, the safest place for a child to ride is in the back seat. Children over 40 pounds should ride in a booster seat until the vehicle's lap and shoulder belts fit properly. (Never place the shoulder belt under your child's arm or behind her back.) You should never allow your child to ride in the cargo bed of a truck, nor should you ever leave her alone in an automobile, especially on hot days; young children are particularly susceptible to heat exposure and dehydration.

In the kitchen. Preschoolers love to help mom and dad cook. And it can be fun to have a small sous chef, as long as you play it safe. Be extra vigilant about repeating basic rules—never touch the stove, never grab something from on top of the stove, never open the oven. Be sure always to place pots on the back burner with handles turned toward the rear of the stovetop, and be especially careful with hot liquids, hot cooking utensils, and splattering grease, all of which can cause serious burns.

During meals. Preschoolers are always in a hurry, and chewing food can seem like a big waste of time. Although a child can choke on just about anything, there are a number of especially hazardous foods for children younger than five. Avoid these foods or cut them into small chunks (not coin-size pieces) and keep an eye on your child as she eats them: nuts, hard candies, raw carrots, popcorn, and grapes.

On bikes. By this age, most children have mastered the tricycle and some may be daring enough to totter off on a two-wheeler. Before your child gets on any bike, check the brakes and make sure she knows how to use them. Choose a bike with rubber-coated pedals rather than slippery plastic ones, and make sure the bike is the right size for her and properly adjusted. (Buying one she'll grow into could set her up for disaster.) Buy a snug but comfortable helmet and insist that your child wear it every time she rides. Children this age shouldn't ride in the roadway without supervision.

At the playground. Preschoolers can handle most playground equipment with ease. But falls happen. Here's what to look for in a safe playground:

- There should be a protective surface under play equipment that is soft enough to absorb a fall—a rubber mat or 12 inches of sand, sawdust, or wood chips—and it should extend 6 feet in all directions from stationary equipment.
- Play structures should be at least 12 feet apart.
- The space between ladder rungs and guardrails should be less than 3½ inches or more than 9 inches, and all elevated surfaces should have guardrails.
- Equipment shouldn't have any protruding pieces or sharp edges.
- Routine maintenance should be performed at the playground on a regular basis.

Guns. Children this age love to imitate Mom and Dad, which makes homes with firearms especially hazardous. In fact, children who live in homes that have guns are more likely to be shot by themselves, friends, or family members than injured by an intruder. Ideally, you should keep guns—especially handguns, which are easy for small children to manipulate—out of your house. If you *do* have a gun, store it unloaded and in a locked place separate from the ammunition.

Bunk beds. Children love them, but they do pose certain dangers. To prevent falls, children younger than six should never sleep on the top bunk—even with a guardrail. The gap between the side rail and guardrail should be no more than 3½ inches.

To prevent collapse, don't allow children to jump or play on either bunk. Place the beds in a corner of the room so there are walls on two sides for support and be sure the supportive wires or slats under the mattresses are secure and that the mattresses fit snugly.

In the bath. It may be tempting to sneak away for a minute or two, but preschoolers still require supervision when they're in the tub, because they can drown in just a few inches of water.

Crossing streets. Preschoolers don't have the concentration or common sense to know when it's safe to cross the street. It's important to go through the look-both-ways drill every time you're out together, but don't expect your child to be able to handle that responsibility on her own until at least age seven.

CONFLICT
Desire for greater control versus physical and emotional readiness

Now that your child is coming into her own as a small, fairly competent person, she's going to want to be treated like one—*all the time* (except when she wants to be babied). The trouble is, there are still many skills that lie just beyond the limits of her ability. Buttoning buttons. Tying shoes. Crossing the street. Cutting with a knife. As an adult, you have the life experience and intellectual ability to forecast disaster in numerous "I-want-to-do-it-myself" situations. You know, for instance, that allowing your child to crack an egg without your help will mean that you're going to be cleaning a gloppy mess off the floor. But your child isn't burdened by any concerns about her physical limitations. She still believes that if she wants to do something, well, that means she can. Whether you let her fumble along on her own or try to help her with the more difficult (or dangerous) tasks, her reaction is likely to be the same: frustration—sometimes complete with screaming, kicking, and flailing on the floor.

Certain routines, like getting dressed, are likely to become areas of conflict during the next two years as your child develops strong ideas about what she wants to wear. This doesn't have so much to do with a true fashion sense (as you'll undoubtedly realize, when she repeatedly insists on wearing a striped shirt with plaid pants) as a desire to exert her newfound independence. Her choices, whether they be princess outfits or cowboy boots, are an attempt to tell the world who she is—today, anyway. Because her imagination is so vivid these days, don't be surprised if your child goes through a stage or two of wanting to dress like a character in a movie or book. She's simply trying out different personas, in an attempt to find which one suits her best.

Striking the delicate balance between allowing your child to be independent but not expecting too much can be tricky. And your child is almost always likely to overestimate her abilities. Now that she's walking so well, for instance, she'll resist riding in a stroller for long walks or hikes. What you may find, however, is that, while she sets off eagerly, she'll poop out somewhere along the way and get tired and cranky. In an instant, your autonomous, self-reliant child can revert to babyhood, crying and insisting she wants to be carried. Planning ahead and recognizing your child's limitations can go a long way toward averting disaster.

Don't be surprised if your child goes through phases in which her physical abilities seem to falter, when her hands seem to tremble as she builds a tower of blocks, or her normally confident stride seems hesitant and uncertain. The march toward greater competency isn't necessarily a linear one, and backward steps may reflect her ambivalence about growing up, especially if these phases are accompanied by clingy, whiny behavior. In general, such blips in the learning curve aren't a cause for concern, but they are your tip-off that your child is going through an insecure, needy phase. Take them as your cue to tune into your child emotionally and to provide a little extra love and reassurance.

How it feels to be me

I can't believe all the stuff I can do! It used to take me forever to walk up and down the stairs, and it was hard for me to figure out how to put on my own shirt. Now I can do lots of things for myself, and that makes me feel really good, especially when I can see how proud it makes you. In fact, one of the best things about being able to do all these new things is showing you that I can do them! I love it when you watch me run my fastest or climb on the jungle gym, or draw a picture. When you smile and tell me I did a good job, it's about the best feeling in the world. I could do it over and over again.

Sometimes I get mad at you because you aren't paying as much attention to me as you used to. When I was falling down a lot and doing naughty things like drawing on the walls with my crayons, you were always right there. Now that I'm such a big person you leave me alone more and get distracted with other things, like talking on the phone and making dinner. If I'm playing a game or having fun on my own, I don't mind so much. But sometimes I get scared and feel really alone, and then I want you to be with me and make me feel

YOU AND YOUR CHILD
How your child's new skills affect you

The burden of parenting becomes noticeably lighter as children mature into capable preschoolers. No longer do you have to hover every moment of every day, worrying that your child is going to crack her head open on the coffee table or fall down the stairs. (Sure, it could still happen. But it's not nearly as likely.) That said, there's still plenty to do. In fact, you're going to face some new challenges in the next two years.

Because you've got a novice on your hands, everything your child does is going to be at a slower pace than you—unless it's faster, which is to say that children this age march to the beat of better. If you're not there right away, it can make me very upset. I know you want to talk on the phone, but I want your attention, too!

I love going to preschool like the big kids. We have lots of fun during the day, and I get to play with my friends. But I miss you, and sometimes I worry that you may not come to get me. That scares me! I'm starting to learn that you always do pick me up, and, boy, am I glad about that.

Usually I feel pretty tired by the end of the day. I like to run around so much, it's hard to know when to stop. When I'm tired, I sometimes need you to help me slow down. I like it when we do the same thing every night, like take a bath, brush our teeth, change into pajamas, and read a book. That helps me feel sleepy. And I still love to snuggle in your lap or on the bed. That makes me feel safe and protected and helps me quiet down. I know I can get cranky and sometimes I even say mean things, like "I hate you." But you're still the most important person to me, and, even though I love my new friends, spending time with you is my very favorite thing.

their own drummers, and that beat is rarely the same as yours. When your child is getting dressed, or putting toothpaste on her toothbrush, or signing her name on a birthday card, you may feel like you've entered some alternate universe, where everything happens in slow motion. In a sense, you have. Although your child is much more adept at these skills than she used to be, she still has to take her time to get it right. You're going to have to tap into reservoirs of patience you might not have known you possessed in order to get through some of these tortuous exercises.

It may help to put yourself in your child's shoes. Think about the last time you tried to program the VCR or assemble a train set. You read the directions, then tried to perform step one. It didn't work.

You went back to the directions and tried again. And again. And again. So it is with a preschooler, whose new skills include, well, just about everything. Add to that the fact that a preschooler's sense of time is somewhat—okay *completely*—nonexistent, and you have a situation that's ripe for combustion. As she's methodically pulling on and adjusting (and readjusting) her socks, and you're watching the seconds tick by wondering just how late you're going to be for work or school, take a deep breath. Find something else to do. Make sure the lunches are packed or the juice cups are filled or her jacket is in her backpack. Unless you're pushed against a wall and have to leave this second, don't step in and do it for your child. It will make her feel bad, and you'll be taking away an opportunity for her to learn. In addition, you may get locked into a power struggle that will make you even later. The fact is, each time she successfully pulls those socks on by herself, she'll get a little better at it, and with time, she'll be able to do it as quickly and easily as you can.

Then there is the other universe—the one where you're the tortoise and she's the hare. The portal to this universe is usually a dangerous place—a parking lot, a crowded department store, a busy street. One minute, your child is standing next to you, the next minute, she's gone. Those able little legs can move quickly when they want to, which almost always seems to be when you *don't* want them to. Pair the natural curiosity of a preschooler with her newfound proficiency with walking and talking, and you'll see why keeping your child close to you in public just became more difficult.

Fortunately, rules loom large at this age. It's time to get in touch with your inner disciplinarian and start laying down rules that will prevent your child from ditching you at the park or dashing across a dangerous parking lot to get to a toy store. Simple, straightforward rules, such as "You must hold my hand in the parking lot," repeated hundreds of times seem to work best.

In situations where your child's safety is at stake, it's important that your will prevails. In other situations, let her win. You're not going to raise a spoiled child by letting her have her way some of the time. In fact, giving her the opportunity to make choices about her life—does she want waffles or oatmeal for breakfast? does she want to go to the park or to the library?—will help her learn how to make decisions. And giving your child plenty of opportunities to exert her new sense of independence, to use her new skills, and to try out her fancy new wings will make both of your lives run more smoothly and happily.

If your child...	Do say	Don't say
can't get her shirt on	"Sure you can. Here, let me turn it right side out for you."	"I'll do it for you."
wants to wear striped pants with a plaid shirt	"Okay" (if you're not going anywhere special), or "Those are both great choices, but they don't go that well together. Can you find a plain shirt to match the pants?"	"No way! You have about as much fashion sense as your father!"
wants to pour her own cereal	"Okay. I'll eat that one and get you a new bowl."	"Just hurry up and eat.'"
wants to lift a bag of groceries	"That bag is pretty heavy. Why don't you help me, because you're so strong."	"No, you can't. It's way too heavy."

Dealing with your ambivalence

As you watch your child mature, it's natural to experience a wide range of emotions. One day you'll wish you could freeze her in time and have her remain a preschooler forever. Other days you'll wish she'd grow up already, so you can have a bigger dose of that sweet freedom you've had a taste of lately.

Vacillating between those two sentiments is normal and actually will help you provide a healthy balance of independence and protection for your child. When you're going through a fearful phase, worrying about every step your child takes toward greater autonomy, it can help to remind yourself that this is a natural response to the letting go that characterizes this period. Likewise, when you're feeling antsy for your little one to move on, it's important to understand that she needs to greet the world at her own pace, in her own way, and that her neediness is actually fairly fleeting in the long-term commitment of parenthood. If you try to enjoy those needy phases while they last, you'll feel comfortable celebrating the bursts of independence that are sure to follow.

HELPING YOUR CHILD GROW
Nurturing competence

As your child gently pushes her way out of the chrysalis of babyhood to emerge as a full-blown child, there are two ways you can aid her mission: by helping her find solutions to the inevitable problems and frustrations that come with learning so many new skills at once, and by slowly giving her the opportunity to take more responsibility for herself and for the family. Here are some of the best ways you can help:

Teach your child a step-by-step approach to new skills. It's easier to tackle a new project when you break it down into small, manageable components—whether you're a small child or a full-grown adult. Think about each step that goes into doing even very simple tasks, then walk her through them step by step. When your child is learning to get a drink of water for herself, for instance, teach her to first pull a step stool or chair up to the sink, get out a plastic cup (have some in an easy-to-reach cupboard so she can manage this without your help), turn on the water so it's flowing in a gentle stream, pick up the cup, stick it under the water for a second or two, set it down, turn off the water, step down off the stool, and grab the cup. Likewise, it can help to lay out her clothing in front of her so she can see how it goes on and teach her tricks, like the tag-in-back and zipper-in-front rules. By buying kid-friendly clothing—pants with elastic waistbands, shoes with Velcro closures, jackets with zippers rather than buttons—you'll give her the best chance at putting them on by herself.

Deal with frustration. Inevitably, there are going to be times when your child hits a wall. She wants to button that button but she can't quite get it or she's trying to tape ears on her paper bunny, but the paper keeps moving at the last minute. Your child's temperament will play a big role in how she handles such situations. Children who are quick to feel defeated and have a low boiling point will struggle more than those who have more patience and a laid-back demeanor. Even if your child falls into the latter category, from time to time she may dissolve into frustrated tears (or worse)—angry both at herself, for not having full command over her body, and at you, for no longer doing everything for her. At times like this, you'll be tempted to rush in and take over for your child. Don't. You can point her in the right direction, but don't do it for her. Instead, talk to her about why she feels angry or frustrated and about what she can do to fix the situation. By giving her words for her feelings and brainstorming with her about solutions, you'll teach her how to handle future frustrations. And, by paying attention to the situations that trigger your child's frustration, you may even be able to divert tantrums and dodge major confrontations by switching to another activity or distracting her with a new topic of conversation.

Overcome toilet-teaching problems. Even kids who learned to use the potty when they were two may have an accident now and again. But that's just exactly what they are: accidents. These don't call for punishment, but rather understanding and compassion. The truth is, children this age sometimes get so caught up in what they're doing that they simply forget to go or put it off until it's too late. To prevent future mishaps, have her help you clean up the mess and change her clothes (and then carefully wash her hands), and remind her as she's playing to take a potty break.

Bed-wetting is common at this age, too. Some children are such deep sleepers that they aren't roused by the need to go to the bathroom. Others may be afraid to get up in the night by themselves or have such small bladders that they can't make it through the night without urinating. Get your child into the habit of going to the bathroom just before she gets in bed, and limit her fluids during the hour preceding bedtime if wetting is a real problem. When she has an accident, try to take a matter-of-fact attitude. Scolding your child can make her feel ashamed or anxious, both of which may actually increase the likelihood of future incidents. If your child seems to have lots of accidents, have your pediatrician check her for physical problems, like a urinary tract infection.

Bowel control should be good by this age, but some children grapple with soiling as well. Ironically, the most common cause for this is constipation. Stool retention is most common between the ages of two and five, when children are struggling with independence and control. If a bowel movement is painful, your child may develop a fear of going. When she avoids using the bathroom for several days in a row, she eventually will reach a point where she can no longer hold it, and she'll end up going in her pants. If your child has soiling problems, make sure she eats plenty of high-fiber foods, like prunes, peas, and beans, and gets in the habit of trying to move her bowels every day after breakfast. If the problem continues, consult your pediatrician, who may prescribe a stool softener.

Give your child responsibility. Giving your child simple jobs to do around the house can increase her sense of self-confidence and competence. Let her feed the cat or set the table or put away her toys at night. Praise her efforts, even if she doesn't accomplish the task the way an adult would, and show her how to finish the job. By giving her the opportunity to contribute to the family, you'll show her you see her as dependable and capable, which will make her more likely to grow into that type of person.

Balance the novel and the familiar. As your child ventures further afield in her quest for independence, it's important to maintain a balance between new experiences and familiar ones. Visiting new places, trying different activities, and meeting people all can challenge children to explore and learn and foster their growth as individuals. Too much novelty, however, can be overwhelming, making your child feel fearful, clingy, and small. As you plan your daily activities, do so with an eye toward mixing new experiences with the known and familiar, which give your child a sense of security, self-confidence, and trust in the world.

Let's talk!

Your three- to four-year-old's communication skills

Two-year-olds are geared for action. They love to do things, and they're always busy. Although your child won't lose his tendency toward constant motion once he's three, he will slow down somewhat as a new, exciting talent emerges and captures his imagination: the gift of gab.

While two-year-olds learn to name many things—banana, chair, playground—and to form simple two- to three-word sentences, three-year-olds begin to tackle the building blocks of true communication, using syntax, structure, and style to form increasingly complex sentences. During the preschool years, your child will begin using language in more sophisticated ways. He can express his needs and desires more clearly ("I'm thirsty. Could I have a glass of water?"); express his emotions ("When you said 'Hurry up!' that hurt my feelings"); and work out problems with peers ("Here, you can play with that bunny while I play with this one").

It's actually pretty remarkable, but by age four, most children have the fundamentals of grammar down pat—putting an *s* on the end of words to make them plural, adding an *ed* to the end of a verb to make it past tense, using personal pronouns like *I* and *you* correctly, and using the negative construction in sentences ("I don't want to go to bed!"). They may still overgeneralize some rules—as in "I sitted in my chair"—but they'll start to recognize and correct even those irregular constructions in the coming months.

More complicated sentence structures may still confuse children this age, however. The passive voice construction ("The cat's food was eaten by the dog") and out-of-order sequences ("Before we go to the park we need to clean up this mess") will enter his speech over the next several years.

Despite its complexities and difficulties, language is like a fun new toy for children this age. Now is a great time to introduce your child to simple word games, like rhyming. It may mystify you, but there's nothing more hilarious to a preschooler than rhyming nonsense words. Say "buffle, tuffle, wuffle," for instance, and you're likely to elicit peals of laughter from your child and launch him into a day-long exploration of words that rhyme with *ruffle*. It's a classic example of play with a purpose. Repetitive rhymes, nursery rhymes, songs, and chants are some of the best ways to get your child used to forming new sounds, and such games actually help prepare and organize his mind for the growth of language.

DEVELOPMENTAL MILESTONE
Building language

The metamorphosis from a physical being into a verbal one doesn't occur overnight, but gradually you'll notice changes. Instead of stealing a toy from another child, your child will ask for it (and maybe even say "please," a favorite word with kids this age). Instead of throwing himself on the floor when he doesn't get his own way, he'll yell, "I'm mad at you!" or even, "I hate you!" At first blush, the latter may not seem like progress. But it is. When you think about the self-control it takes to channel that preschool fury through his mouth rather than his fists, you'll understand how much your child has grown up—and how hard he is trying to abide by adult ("No hitting!") rules of behavior.

Your child will love to talk to you at this age, but he'll also spend lots of time talking to himself. Some children spout a near-constant stream-of-conscious narration as they go about their day. Whereas a two-year-old might ask you to help him find his teddy bear, a three-year-old is just as likely to coach himself through the process by parroting the words you usually use: "Where's my teddy? Is he under the bed? No, he's not there. Is he in the closet? No . . ." and so on. (When he can't find it, then he'll ask you to help him.)

You may find this barrage of muttering worrisome. Actually, it's just the opposite. Children talk to themselves to direct their actions and work through tasks on their own. This kind of "inner speech" (although it's still technically outer speech at this age) may even help create important neurological connections in the brain that will help your child make decisions and focus his attention, a critical task at this age. In fact, studies show that young children perform tasks more effectively when they talk themselves through their actions.

Gradually, your child's self-talk will become internal, and he'll learn to think—rather than speak—his way through tasks large and small. In the meantime, it's important to remember that your child's chatter is simply evidence of a mind that's hard at work.

The age of "Why?"

Preschoolers not only discover that language is a great way to communicate, but they also begin to realize it's a wonderful way to learn, and their eager, open minds are like learning machines.

They absorb lots of what you say and do, but they always want more information, which is why the favorite word of many preschoolers is *why*. You'll get dozens of "why?" questions daily for the next couple of years, and it can get wearing, but consider this: The fact that a three-year-old is capable of asking, say, "Why can birds fly and I can't?" is itself fairly extraordinary. A year ago, it never would have occurred to him to ask.

When you can feel your patience becoming a bit threadbare, it's important to remind yourself that questioning things is the way your child learns to, well, learn. The ability to ask questions and absorb the answers is the foundation of learning and will help him not only in his umpteen years of future schooling but also in virtually every aspect of life.

To aid and encourage your child's quest for knowledge, you should strive to reward his natural curiosity with attentive, thoughtful answers—even if sometimes the answer is, "That's a good question. I don't know why the sky is blue." Because your child may come up with many questions that test the limits of your knowledge, it's a good idea to invest in a children's encyclopedia, which can provide you with concise, child-friendly information on hundreds of topics of interest to kids. Showing your child where to go for more information and the method by which it is organized (alphabetically), will also teach him how to discover the answers to his questions himself once he is capable—a skill that will serve him well for the rest of his life.

Keep in mind that sometimes incessant "why" questions are simply your child's attempt to hold your attention and carry on a rudimentary (often meaningless) conversation. You'll probably be able to tell the difference between this faux questioning, which typically is more distracted and less serious, and the real thing. Even this less insistent form of questioning has a purpose, however. By indulging him (if you have the time and patience) you give him the opportunity to practice the back-and-forth of real conversation and give him what he craves—your undivided attention.

If your child...	Do say	Don't say
says she hates her baby sister	"It's hard when the baby needs so much attention, isn't it?"	"That's a terrible thing to say! You don't hate your sister."
says, "You're mean"	"You're angry because you want to wear your Batman shirt to the park, aren't you?"	"Yeah? Well I think you're the one who is being mean."
says, "Why do I have to drink my milk?"	"Because milk helps make your bones big and strong."	"Because I said so."
says, "I runned to the store"	"Yes, you ran fast, didn't you?"	"No, honey, you ran to the store."
says, "I can't turn the thingie on the door"	"That knob is hard to turn, isn't it?"	"That thingie is hard to turn."

CONFLICT
It's easier to hit than to explain why you're angry

It shouldn't come as any surprise that preschoolers are still learning the delicate art of self-control. You don't have to look any farther than the highway during rush hour to realize that many adults still struggle with this task. So, when your child is overcome by rage, fear, or unhappiness, don't be shocked if he reverts to more physical means of expressing himself.

To help him keep outbursts in check, give him words for his emotions—tools to express the sometimes confusing tumult of feelings raging inside him. Helping your child label his emotions will increase his level of self-awareness and self-control and give him more confidence. The truth is, his own anger may be quite frightening to him. Children are magical thinkers, remember, and he may believe that thinking bad thoughts about you will make them come true. Naming his emotions can take away some of the fear by letting him know how universal his feelings are.

You don't need to wait for high-intensity situations to get your child acquainted with his emotions. When he is in a goofy, giggly mood, you can say, "You're happy to be coloring today, aren't you?" When he stomps his foot, say, "It looks like you're feeling frustrated that you can't get that zipper started." By identifying not only what he's feeling but why he may be feeling it, you help your child understand the source of his misery, which can be comforting. You can even tell him about a time when you were sad or frustrated— "When I was learning to drive a stick shift car, I got so frustrated it made me feel like crying," for instance. Sharing a personal experience will make your child feel better about his woes, and let him know how normal—and common—such emotions are.

Acting out emotions can also help your child link words with feelings. Ask him to show you what sad or happy looks like, or, when you're angry, you could even lighten the situation by saying, "See my face? That's what mad looks like."

Some children express their emotions easily. Others need guidance. To help your child open up, encourage him to tell you what he's feeling. Questions like, "Are you mad? Do you need a hug?" can help your child identify and verbalize the emotions bubbling inside him. If you create an environment in which he feels comfortable talking about his feelings, and reward his efforts by responding with sensitivity, he's more likely to continue the behavior.

Sometimes words won't be enough for your child. When he is very angry and ready to boil over, it can help to show him how to blow off some steam physically—by punching a pillow, running around the yard, or pounding a wad of modeling clay. You'll teach him that physical exertion is a good way to calm himself (something we all need to remember), and give him an indispensable tool for becoming a well-adjusted, emotionally healthy person.

How it feels to be me

It's so much easier for me to say things now that I sometimes want to talk all the time. There were so many things I wanted to know about when I was younger, but I didn't know how to ask. Now that I can ask questions, I do it all the time. I love when you tell me about stuff, like flowers and worms and dinosaurs and trucks. It makes me feel like a big kid to talk to you, and I can't believe how much there is to know!

Now that I can tell you what I want, I make sure to tell you exactly what I want, whenever I think of anything—"I want juice, I want a new doll, I want to go to the park." It feels really good to be able to say what I'm thinking. It makes me mad when you don't do what I want, though, and when I get mad I may need you to remind me to use my words. Sometimes I just forget! Or I might even say mean things, but I always feel bad afterward, and I usually feel better after I say I'm sorry.

I like to sound like you, so lots of the time I say just what you say, even if I don't know exactly what it means. I'm like that bird called a parrot. I just repeat what I hear, which sometimes makes people laugh.

I also love to say silly things and sing silly songs, and it makes me very happy when you and I do it together. Talking is so much fun!

YOU AND YOUR CHILD
Communicating with each other

Now that you can hear what's going on in your child's mind, you may wonder how you ever got along without his input. He can tell you he has an earache or that he's scared or, best of all, that he loves you. What bliss! And now that he can understand almost everything you say (provided you put it in preschooler-ese) you can begin to connect with each other in a whole new way. Here are some things you can do to facilitate parent-child communication:

Ask your child questions. General questions, like "How was your day?" are too broad for children this age and are likely to elicit one-word answers—"Fine," for instance. But if you zero in on specific information ("Did you color a picture at school today?") you may release a flood of information, not only about art projects but about playground activities, friends, and circle time. When your child responds to your questions, let him know you heard what he said by repeating it back to him and asking an appropriate follow-up question. Doing so will reinforce the idea that conversation includes a back-and-forth exchange and get him used to the idea of pursuing a topic through to its logical conclusion.

Listen when your child talks. Even if he's stumbling and stuttering, don't rush him or interrupt, and let him know how much you enjoy hearing what he has to say. Being distracted or uninterested may make your child feel that what he has to say is dull or inadequate in some way.

Tell your child stories. Relating what you did during the day—standing in a long line at the grocery store or talking to Grandma—will show your child how to share everyday information. Give him ample opportunity to ask you questions about your activities and respond with thoughtful, unhurried answers. Remember: Repetition helps your child understand things, so he may ask you the same question several times before he's satisfied with the answer.

Dealing with chatter
As wonderful as it is to have a verbal child, there will be times when you long for silence, peace, and calm, none of which is likely to occur in the presence of a preschooler. After the zillionth "Why?"

of the day, you may feel like pulling a Greta Garbo and screaming, "I vant to be alone!" Although your child may need solitude, too, he's not likely to understand at this age why you need it. You can try to explain that you're in a quiet mood and would like a few minutes to think about something, but that may backfire by making him anxious and more apt to pester you. Also, avoid pejorative phrases, like "chatterbox" or "motormouth," which can make your child feel ashamed of his desire to express himself.

You are more likely to succeed by distracting your child with a game or activity. Get out his crayons or dolls, sing a song or nursery rhyme, or offer to read him a book. If you're truly desperate for some quiet, get in the car and go for a drive. Children often retreat into their own imaginary worlds as they ride, and it can buy you a few moments of hard-won serenity.

HELPING YOUR CHILD GROW
Creating a language-rich environment

Helping your child formulate the right words will be beneficial to him in every aspect of his life. There's no more important tool for education or socialization than language, and parents play a pivotal role in helping their children blossom as verbal creatures. Here are some things you can do to assist your child's language development:

Encourage your child to talk as he goes about his daily activities. Urge him to talk through situations before taking action. Ask him to describe what's happening as he plays—"What did your doll buy at the store?" or "Why are there steps up to that tower?"

Model appropriate language skills. Use proper grammar and let your child observe grown-up conversations, which will teach him the rules of communication.

Include your child in family conversations. Let him carry messages between family members. For instance, if you say to your child, "Ask Daddy if he knows where I can find the keys," you're making him an important link in family communication and teaching him to remember things he hears.

Play with words and language. Sing songs, make up rhymes, and repeat tongue twisters, all of which will help your child achieve better verbal fluency, help his later listening and reading skills, and teach him the joy of using words.

Don't drill your child on vocabulary or grammar. Language skills grow most quickly in the course of everyday interactions.

Read to your child every day. Hearing stories helps children understand numerous concepts, like sequences of events, grammar, and dialogue, and talking about what's happening in the pictures can expand your child's vocabulary and his grasp of the versatility of language.

Talk about things as you do them. As you go about your daily activities, it can be helpful for you to adopt a childlike approach to conversation, narrating your actions and explaining why you're doing them. Some of the information may go over your child's head. But listening to your words and the structure of your sentences will help your child become a successful communicator much more quickly than in a household in which "silence is golden."

When your child wants something, encourage him to use words. If he whines, points, or cries, gently remind him, "It's much easier to simply tell Mommy or Daddy what you want."

Encourage him to ask you not just those "why" questions he loves so much, but also how, when, and where. It takes lots of practice for children to understand how to correctly ask and answer such queries.

Use prepositions. To foster your child's grasp of these words, take every opportunity to show him how they are used: "I thought I put my keys *on* the table, but look—they fell *under* the table."

Tell stories. Children love to make up stories at this age, but it can be helpful for them to repeat the plot of a book or TV show, too. It teaches them not only how to put words in an appropriate sequence but also how to order events.

Use the names of household objects and point out things while you are driving or walking. "See the dump truck? I wonder where it's going to take that load of dirt."

Don't be afraid to introduce new words or concepts. "That truck is called a backhoe." "This big dinosaur is a diplodocus." "When you meet someone new, it's nice to say 'How do you do?'" Children thrive when they're gently pushed to expand their knowledge.

Encourage your child to talk to others. Your child can respond to the checker in the grocery store who asks him a question or the neighbor who says hello, for example. The more confident he feels about expressing himself, the more capable he will be of handling social interactions with his peers and teachers. To nudge him in the right direction without pressuring him, explain to him that it's polite to respond when other people ask him a question or greet him. You can even practice with stuffed animals to show him how to interact. Then, when you're out in public and someone speaks to your child, say, "Mrs. Klein said hello. Would you like to say hello back?" If he hesitates, don't push it. But show your child how to respond by being friendly yourself. The surest way to teach him social skills is to model them for him on a daily basis.

Build quiet time into every day. The brain needs restful periods to assimilate new information and form neural connections.

Dealing with stuttering and other speech problems

An estimated 4 to 10 percent of children stutter, a problem that's more likely to afflict boys, but many children go through a minor phase of stammering as their language growth progresses. Causes vary, but usually it does not indicate any underlying developmental problems. Sometimes children have simply learned too many words in a short time period and are groping to find the right one. Other times, stuttering is caused by his young mind moving faster than his tongue. Stuttering can become more pronounced when children are sick, tired, excited, or anxious.

Although stuttering is likely to make you worry, it shouldn't. Most cases of stuttering go away on their own within about a year. In fact, it's more likely to clear up quickly if you ignore it. Don't finish your child's sentences for him or rush him as he struggles to get out a word or phrase. Such tactics tend to backfire, making your child self-conscious about his speech and anxious about speaking quickly and fluently.

Slowing down the pace of your speech will let your child see that he doesn't have to master rapid-fire speech to be like a grown-up and help him feel more relaxed about the pace of his own communicating.

If your child's stuttering is severe (he twitches and grimaces as he tries to speak) and long-lasting (more than a few months), however, ask your pediatrician to recommend a good speech and language specialist.

Most children sort out correct pronunciation during the preschool years or shortly after, but many three-year-olds still will find the sounds "r," "th," "s," "sh," "l," "t," "ch," and "j" difficult to master. Give it time. Most speech problems are self-correcting once the child is capable of recognizing the error and has the verbal dexterity to correct it. If your child hasn't mastered intelligible speech by age three, however, see your doctor to rule out any physical problems. If nothing is diagnosed, consult a speech or language therapist, who can help sort out the problem before your child gets into school.

What I know

Your three- to four-year-old's intellectual growth

From the moment your child wakes up in the morning to the moment she closes her eyes at night, she is absorbing information about the world. She observes that the moon changes shape, that plants grow and wither, that her tummy rumbles when she's hungry. As a toddler, she learned largely by doing things—filling a bucket with sand taught her about weight and mass, and walking downstairs taught her about distance and movement (and gravity!). Now, your inquisitive little one is expanding her world not just by actions, which remain a high point at this age, but by talking about things as well.

Her incessant "Why?" questions are proof not only of her curiosity but of her increased ability to digest and understand simple bits of information. She asks questions because she's ready for answers.

She'll learn by talking to you, to teachers, and even to peers. Preschoolers love to show how much they know, and it's not unusual for children to come home from a play date brimming with new information gleaned from their pint-size companions: "Alex says those bugs that curl up when you touch them are called pill bugs." "Misha told me that when you mix red and blue it makes purple!"

Preschoolers also learn from their experiences, from their observations, from things they overhear, from shows they see on TV. As their brains' neural networks expand and change, they'll begin to make connections between new experiences and things they've done previously. With just a few short years behind her, your child is beginning to build a repertoire of knowledge that will provide a foundation for all her future learning.

DEVELOPMENTAL MILESTONE
Thinking symbolically

Your child's verbal prowess is the most overt proof of her intellectual development, but her ability to think is growing and changing right along with her expanding vocabulary. Most important, she can now discuss events, objects, and people that aren't right in front of her— she can tell you about what happened when she was out with the baby-sitter, describe the witch in her dream, or pretend to talk to Daddy on the telephone. That change marks a critical shift in her intellectual development, one that propels her by a giant leap from babyhood to the world of big kids. Your child has become a symbolic thinker rather than a physical one, a stage she'll be in until she's about seven years old, when she'll take another quantum leap into the world of logic and reason.

As preschoolers become able to think symbolically, they also will begin linking specific pieces of information into patterns. Your child may observe, for instance, that four pencils are arranged from smallest to largest; that ants, grasshoppers, and beetles are all bugs; or that the sky, a swimming pool, and her shirt are all light blue. Her progress in this area is a good sign. The ability to see relationships between sometimes disparate objects can help your child organize her thoughts and ideas, which will help her process new information more efficiently and express herself more clearly.

Because she can now hold images in her head, your child is able to connect new events with old ones—"We're going to go to a puppet show, like the one we saw last month about the dogs"—which makes explaining things easier for you and understanding things easier for her. She also can enjoy a sense of anticipation about upcoming events, like going to see a friend, visiting a favorite museum, or eating a well-loved food, because she can conjure the feeling of what it was like the last time she experienced it.

You'll be amazed by the things your preschooler is able to remember. She'll mention an event that happened a year ago, tell you the name of a child she met—once!—at the park several months ago, or recite an entire (short) book from memory. When you realize how sharp her memory is, you may find it frustrating that she doesn't seem to be able to recall where she left her teddy bear or juice cup. The trouble is, while her memory works very well, she doesn't understand how to use it yet. If you show her how to access her mental storage banks—"Think about where you were when you had your teddy bear last"—she'll slowly start to get the hang of it. But don't expect miracles. Most children don't start developing true memory strategies until about age six.

Along with her amazing memory, your preschooler has made enormous strides in her ability to concentrate. Whereas a year ago, she might not have sat through a whole book or would wander around during circle time at day care or preschool, these days she's able to sit still for long periods of time, depending on her temperament and how interested she is in the project at hand. She has the patience to draw a detailed picture, build an elaborate structure out of blocks, play an involved game of "house" or superheroes, or sit quietly in the grocery cart (as long as she has something to occupy her attention) while you're shopping.

The building blocks of future learning

As your child's thinking matures, so does her understanding of basic concepts involved in later education like time, counting, and spelling. Children learn at different rates, so don't worry if your neighbor's child can count higher than yours or if your child doesn't seem interested in writing her name. She'll pick up all the necessary skills in time if you continue to provide a rich, open, and stimulating environment. That said, here are some of the intellectual feats most preschoolers can accomplish:

Understanding (loosely) the concept of time. Your child may already know the general progression of a typical 24-hour period— she wakes up, eats breakfast, goes to school, eats lunch—and if she doesn't, she'll get there soon. Preschoolers use lots of words to talk about time, but they may confuse words like *yesterday* and *tomorrow*, and their concept of the actual passage of time and time phrases, like *in an hour* or *two days from now* is still shaky unless you connect it to something concrete. For instance, you could say, "We're going to go to the store in one hour—that's about as long as *Sesame Street*," or buy a big calendar and mark off the days of the week to give her a better sense of duration. She remembers infrequent special occasions like her birthday and major holidays, but the concept of a year is still confusing. Despite her growing understanding of time, your child still lives in the here and now, so her needs and wants have an urgency (her demand for more juice may be uttered in a voice that makes it sound like a true emergency) that is absent in older children.

Counting at least up to ten. As soon as your child catches onto the pattern of numbers, she may even be able to count up to 100!

Preschoolers can do more than simply recite numbers, however. They can actually count objects—sometimes as many as 20 at a time—a feat that was too much for most children even a few months ago. Although you should never push your child to learn more than she's ready for, she may enjoy playing simple math games. Try laying out five pennies, then ask her, "What would happen if we took one away?" The idea is not to have her adding and subtracting before she reaches kindergarten, but to challenge her mind to think about how to manipulate numbers and learn to solve simple problems.

Grasping the concept of letters and writing. Thanks to preschoolers' increased understanding of symbols, your child will soon realize that a written symbol can stand for something in the real world, and she will recognize that the lines and squiggles on a printed page are actually words that tell a story or send a message. In fact, most four-year-olds can identify capital letters and many lowercase letters as well. Although most children aren't reading at this age, one of the most exciting advances for both you and your child will be her ability to write. At some point during the next two years, she'll probably learn to form at least a few letters and may even be able to write her name and simple words like *cat* and *dog*, *mom* and *dad*. Her writing will most likely be big and awkward-looking at this age, and she may go through a stage of writing letters backward—a normal phenomenon for novices who are still trying to sort out this incredibly complicated task. Follow your child's lead, and don't push too hard in this area, tempting though it may be.

Naming colors. Most children this age can identify the colors red, white, blue, green, yellow, orange, pink, purple, black, and brown. (Your child also may have a favorite color—yet another attempt to define herself and set herself apart as an individual.)

Comparing the sizes of things. Preschoolers often love to talk about things that are very small (like them) or very large (like you). Your child can arrange objects from smallest to largest or maybe even lightest to heaviest. But she won't be able to understand that a short, fat glass and a tall, thin glass can hold the same quantity of milk. In her mind, the taller one must hold more, because it is "bigger." The milk-in-the-glass problem requires her to consider more than one factor at the same time, a feat that will be beyond her for a few more years.

Seeing spatial relationships. As your child gradually adds the use of prepositions to her language skills, she'll also gain an understanding of the concepts to which they are linked. In other words, the out-of-sight, out-of-mind attitude that characterizes toddlerhood will begin to disappear during the next two years. During this stage, your child becomes capable of locating a block that fell under the bed (she'll not only be able to think about looking there, she can follow your request to do so) or a juice cup sitting beside the couch.

Is there a problem?

Children develop at different rates. Chances are, if your child hasn't accomplished all the major tasks of this developmental period, she will shortly. But certain behaviors (or lack thereof) do signal the need for an evaluation by your child's doctor. Underlying physical problems— like hearing or vision loss or a chemical imbalance that causes hyperactivity—could interfere with your child's cognitive development. Consult your pediatrician if your child:

- Is unable to concentrate on any activity for more than five minutes
- Doesn't add an s to make words plural or doesn't add an ed to form the past tense
- Can't name any colors
- Can't recognize any letters
- Can't count
- Seems uncomfortable holding a pencil or crayon
- Can't stack at least six blocks
- Doesn't know her first and last name

How it feels to be me

I know how to count and spell my name, and I can sing lots of songs that I learned in preschool. I like to show everyone what I can do—even the guy who works at the gas station and the lady waiting at the bus stop. When they clap and smile, I know I did a good job, which makes me feel really good.

Sometimes I get confused and have to start over, especially when I'm trying to count things, like the raisins on my lunch plate. I have to concentrate really hard or I lose track of what number I was on. After I count them, I sometimes pretend my raisins are little creatures who like to dance around or crazy monsters who get in lots of fights. That makes me laugh hard—so hard that I may forget to eat my lunch.

I can remember lots of things, though, like people's names and the words to songs. Once you told me that I have a mind like a steel trap, but I can't understand how something like a trap could get inside my head. Wouldn't that hurt?

I like knowing lots of things, so when I get interested in something, like dinosaurs or dolls, that's all I want to talk about. Being able to ask you questions is great, and I may think about your answers for a long time afterward. Sometimes it seems like you know everything there is to know about everything, and sometimes it seems like I do, too!

CONFLICT
The limits of understanding

With all your child knows now, it can be easy to overestimate her intellectual capacity. But the reality is, her grasp of the world around her is constrained by certain intellectual shortfalls. For one thing, a preschooler remains fairly egocentric in her viewpoint. Although she may be able to empathize with you if you're feeling sad or tired, she'll continue to see most issues from her own perspective. For instance, she may still be convinced that her teddy bear, dolls, trees, and flowers have feelings or believe that objective events occur to serve her subjective needs—"It's warm out today because I want to go to the park," or "That parking space was open because we want to get ice cream."

Young children also may believe that wishing someone harm will actually cause them to be harmed, which makes your child's bad thoughts about you (she'll have them when you punish her or get angry at her) all the more frightening and upsetting. Realizing how much her anger at you can scare her can help you feel compassion in the face of your own frustration.

Your child tends to think literally, so plays on words—"I'm so hungry I could eat a horse," or "You can run as fast as lightning"— will elicit very literal responses: "You can't really eat a horse, can you?" or "Yeah, I'm as fast as lightning!" Likewise, she still may confuse fantasy and reality for the next couple of years, believing everything from dreams to television shows are real. Talking about pretend situations and real situations can help her sort out the two, and by the time she enters school, she should have a pretty good understanding of what is make-believe and what is not.

YOU AND YOUR CHILD
Being a good teacher

At some point, every parent experiences the joy of seeing the world through her child's eyes. If it hasn't happened already, you're in for a treat. Three- to four-year-olds can help you see everything, from a worm to a tree to the color violet, as if you're looking at it for the first time. They can rejuvenate your love of learning and renew your appreciation for small details that so often slip beneath the radar screens of busy adults' daily lives—the dewdrop on the leaf, the shadow on the sidewalk, the pile of sparkly rocks.

Call these the wonder years, because both you and your child will be immersed in a journey of discovery. As each new experience unfolds before your child's curious eyes, you'll be present to help her understand it, to provide her with words for what she sees, to tell her stories and to share with her information that helps her make sense of it all. Your child looks to you as a teacher, and how you handle this role can go a long way toward fostering a love of learning in your child.

As your child's first teacher, you may find the following advice paradoxical: You don't need to teach her anything. That is, you don't need to sit down and give her a formal lesson. In fact, imposing a formal learning environment might actually discourage your child from wanting to know new things. Your role as teacher is a much more organic one than most of us imagine. As you go about your day, simply answer her questions, point out interesting things, listen to what she says, read her books, and give her plenty

If your child...	Do say	Don't say
makes a mistake while counting to ten	"That was great! Do you want to do it again together?"	"Oops! You missed the number eight. Better try again."
writes her name with some of the letters backward	"You wrote your name! Do you want to try another word if I write it for you first?"	"That's good, but some letters are backward. Let me show you how to do it right."
likes to look at books and pretend she's reading	"Reading is fun, isn't it?"	"Here. Let me teach you how to really read that book"— and launch into a full-scale lesson.
asks, "Which has more sand: the red bucket or the blue one?"	"Let's figure it out. Can you think of a way we could tell which has more?"	"The blue one."

of time and space to play—perhaps the best learning circumstances of all.

When she asks you a question, be clear and concise in your answer. Young children don't need (or want) volumes of information. To make sure you're not giving her more detail than she can handle, watch her reaction to your explanations. When her eyes glaze over, she's had enough. Another way to gauge her comprehension is to ask her to explain something back to you. That way, you'll see how much she understands the concepts behind the words, which will help you fine-tune the information you provide in the future.

Understanding your child's learning style

Children begin exhibiting different learning styles during the preschool years. Some children learn best through language, by talking and reading about issues. Others are mathematical. They love numbers and like to make logical connections between facts. Still others are physical. They're good at sports and dancing and learn best when their whole bodies are involved in the learning process (they might like to dance while they learn their ABCs, for example). Children also can be musical, using rhythm and song to remember things; social, learning best in a group; or spatially oriented, enjoying building structures and taking things apart.

By paying attention to the innate inclinations of your child, you can help her uncover her strengths and enhance her ability to learn by catering to her natural instincts. For instance, if your child is spatially oriented and is having trouble with the alphabet, you could try playing with magnetic letters, which will allow her to conceive of what they're like physically; if your musical child struggles with numbers, you could make up songs about counting.

If it's tough to tell which category your child favors, it can be helpful to consider whether she tends to be a "right brain" or "left brain" thinker. In general, the right hemisphere of the brain looks at the whole picture while the left brain analyzes the details. If your child is more of a doer than a talker, she's probably more "right brained," and vice versa. Children who rely more on their left hemispheres tend to have better language skills than right-hemisphere thinkers, who may be more artistic. Neither style is better or worse. But getting a sense of how your child thinks can help you tailor the information you give her in a way that she'll be most efficient at processing.

No matter which hemisphere your child favors, it's important to engage her in activities that help bridge the two sides of the brain, encouraging them to work in tandem, which will strengthen her ability to comprehend new material. Although the two hemispheres won't be fully harmonized until puberty, it can be beneficial to promote their integration even at this age. Playing a game that includes both a verbal and a visual component, like Simon says, is a great way to get the whole brain involved. Other ideas: Pretend to be a variety of animals, complete with movement and noises; talk about making pie while you measure sand with measuring cups; make up a story about a prince and princess while you build a castle out of blocks; or ask your child to explain how she figured out how to solve a problem, like fitting a peg into a hole or completing a puzzle.

HELPING YOUR CHILD GROW
The power of play

Children are born learners. It doesn't occur to them that new information could be boring or uninteresting. They're eager to learn everything they can, as long as they're not forced or rushed. By giving your child plenty of leeway to play, experiment, create, and get messy, you'll give her the best opportunity to acquire new skills and new knowledge and become a student of life.

Earlier in this chapter, we mentioned that there's no need to sit down and teach your child in a formal, systematic way, but that point bears repeating. Things like flash cards, phonics, and memorization projects are too academic for children this age. Studies of four- to six-year-olds show that children become less creative and more anxious in heavily academic settings. Young children learn most efficiently and have the best attitude toward learning when they are encouraged to learn through play.

When your child paints, draws, creates something with clay or blocks, or pretends to be a superhero, it may not look like she's learning. But our adult definitions of education are far too rigid for young children. Your young painter is learning about color and texture, the builder is taking in information about shape and balance, and the superhero is starting to sort out the concepts of good and evil, strong and weak. During all types of play children learn important skills like concentration and perseverance, develop self-confidence, and master problem-solving skills.

To help your child get the most out of her play experiences, give her a variety of toys, preferably ones that have imaginative uses rather than literal ones—a box and some dolls rather than a fully outfitted doll's house, for instance. She also needs plenty of space, both emotionally and physically, to use them. A child who is constantly worried about making a mess will feel restricted in her play, so let her create chaos for a while (with the caveat that she helps clean up later).

Also, encourage her to talk about what's happening as she plays. Although preschoolers often feel inhibited if a parent is hovering while they're playing, you can check in every once in a while and ask a question about what's going on. Who lives in your castle? What is your baby eating? How did you know that piece would fit into the puzzle right there?

If she asks you to join her in play, do so. Your child will learn how to express herself in a variety of ways by watching how you play, too. Just reign in your urge to direct the play situation. Let your child be in charge of what happens and interject comments or questions that inspire your child to come up with new ideas.

Encouraging problem solving
Giving your child the opportunity to solve problems is one of the best ways to foster her intelligence. Being faced with a problem,

Choosing a preschool

Most children this age love preschool, and there's a reason why: It enables them to interact with their peers in a structured environment. They are given the opportunity to create a variety of projects and have a number of new experiences. And, if the program is a good one, it's all done under the loving, watchful eye of a professional, who can help guide your child on her never-ending quest for greater knowledge.

Because it's important that children learn through playing at this age, you should evaluate your choice of preschools carefully. Although the one with the academic setting may look like what you think of as "school," for early-childhood education, it's not the best. A good preschool should have the following characteristics:

The curriculum
- Learning comes about from firsthand experience. Children should be encouraged to move around the room and use the materials creatively. They should have the opportunity to do art projects, play dress-up, put together puzzles, build with blocks, shape things from clay, and read.
- Children are given plenty of opportunities to contribute to the classroom discussions by relating their own experiences, explaining their art projects, or showing the class special items they've brought from home.
- Children are given time to play both indoors and outdoors.

however, can be a frustrating situation for a young child, whose problem-solving skills are still immature. When confronted with intellectual challenges—a block that won't balance on top of another one, a dress that won't fit over her doll's head—your child is likely to turn to you for help. You'll be tempted to step in and take over, telling your child how to fix the situation. But, in the long run, such an approach won't do your child any favors.

A better way to handle these situations is to encourage your child to find her own solutions by asking questions that can lead her in the right direction. For instance, if she's having trouble stacking a

- Children's daily activities include projects that will hone both their fine motor skills (cutting with scissors, painting with a paintbrush, and putting together puzzles) and their gross motor skills (dancing and climbing on play structures).
- The schedule includes a number of language-focused activities, such as reading, looking at books, and allowing the children to make up their own stories.

The teacher

- Teachers should have professional training in early-childhood education.
- Teachers should have frequent one-on-one contact with each child as well as small- and large-group interactions. The teacher should listen respectfully when a child speaks and offer plenty of praise and encouragement for her projects and verbal efforts. Children this age still need lots of guidance and attention to feel safe and secure. Preschool programs that have a high student-to-teacher ratio can allow a shy or withdrawn child to get lost in the shuffle.
- The teacher must be clear and organized about the daily routine (children feel most secure when they know what to expect), but remain flexible about changing activities when the need arises.
- The teacher should be quick to set limits in situations that require discipline but should never belittle the children or punish them physically.

big block on top of a small one, you could ask your child if there's something else that would make a better base. Preschoolers usually have enough experience that they quickly realize if they widen the base, their structure will be sturdier at the top.

Indulging your child's creative efforts also will help her hone her problem-solving skills. If your child wants to make a book, ask her to tell you a story, have her draw a picture to go along with it, and help her bind the pages. Such original creations will not only give your child a sense of accomplishment, they'll teach her that she can make something from nothing and help her trust her own abilities.

Aiding your child's comprehension

Despite their new grasp of symbols, preschoolers are still fairly concrete thinkers. Your child will understand things best when she experiences them first-hand, so if you want her to tackle a new task, like setting the table, it's best to show her, rather than tell her how to do it. Likewise, if you want to explain an abstract concept, you need to give her an example of how it applies to her own life. For instance, if she wants to know what "love" means, you could say, "Do you know how you feel when you're so happy you want to give me a hug? That's what love feels like."

If you're trying to explain a color, shape, or texture she's not familiar with, it's helpful to show her something similar rather than saying, for example, "An oval is like a stretched out circle," which may still be difficult for her to envision.

Recommended reading

For parents:
- *Discover Your Child's Learning Style: Children Learn in Unique Ways— Here's the Key to Every Child's Learning Success* by Mariaemma Willis and Victoria Kindle-Hodson (Prima Publishing)
- *Playing Smart: A Parent's Guide to Enriching, Offbeat Learning Activities for Ages 4 to 14* by Susan K. Perry (Free Spirit Publishing)
- *Your Child's Growing Mind: A Practical Guide to Brain Development and Learning from Birth to Adolescence* by Jane M. Healy, Ph.D. (Main Street Books)

For children:
- *Counting Crocodiles* by Judy Sierra (Harcourt Brace)
- *Miss Spider's Tea Party: The Counting Book* by David Kirk (Scholastic)
- *Ten Minutes Till Bedtime* by Peggy Rathmann (Putnam Publishing)

Let's pretend

Your three- to four-year-old's fantasy life

Last year, your child's playtime revolved around hands-on toys—pressing the button to hear the dog bark, trying to fit the round peg into different-shaped holes, banging on several pots to hear the varying noises they make. He was gathering information about the world around him and learning to manipulate his environment in a very concrete way. His pretend games were simple and straightforward, and often dictated by his toys. If he had a big toy schoolbus, for instance, he would most likely pretend it was taking kids to school as he moved it along the bedroom floor.

This year, as his imagination begins to take off, he will start to see things not just as they are but as they could be. That schoolbus might be a superfast car for a gang of bad guys or a stroller for a baby or a house for a family of small creatures. He'll create dozens of imaginary scenarios as he plays and stays focused on an activity for extended periods of times. Even if he's not actively playing with a toy, you'll know when he's entered fantasyland by the dreamy, far-off look on his face. When he's alone, his pretend play may be very quiet, interior, and private—so much so that he may stop playing when you enter the room—but when he's with his friends, their games of house or cowboys or school can get quite rambunctious as each child vies for the opportunity to direct the "script" of the play scenario and take the game in new directions.

The independence you've seen in other aspects of his life will suffuse this imaginary play as well. More and more frequently, he'll be content to play by himself while you go about your own activities. Although he may want to know where you are and what you're doing, he'll be willing to spend more time alone with his incredibly entertaining new companion: his own mind.

DEVELOPMENTAL MILESTONE
The wonderful world of make-believe

From an adult perspective, the world of a preschooler is small and confined. Your child tags along with you on errands, plays at the park or in the yard, visits a friend or two, maybe attends nursery school or day care. But from where your child sits, the scope of his universe is quite vast—practically unlimited!—thanks to his extraordinary imagination, which blooms to its fullest during the next two years. Children this age can spend hours immersed in fantasy play, pretending to be superheroes, teachers, mommies, kittens, and dinosaurs.

Preschoolers act out and relive events they see on TV or experience in real life, and they create completely new scenarios in which unexpected, outrageous, or magical things occur. A stick becomes a sword with which to slay dragons, a roasting pan becomes a bassinet for a baby doll, a rubber band is transformed into a beautiful bracelet, a slingshot turns into a guitar string.

Why does a child's imagination soar during the preschool years? Fantasy actually plays a critical role in your child's cognitive growth and development, helping him to process and understand the confusing, frightening, and vast amount of information that comes at him during the day. The value of pretend play extends to nearly every aspect of his life. Here are some of the ways fantasy supports your child's growth:

Emotionally. Young children may be overwhelmed by their own emotions as well as by those expressed by friends, parents, siblings, and teachers. By playing out their frustrations, fears, anger, and joy within the safe confines of make-believe scenarios, they begin to put feelings in perspective and understand them in context. If you become angry at your child for making a mess right after you have cleaned his room, for instance, you might hear him parrot your words—"How could you?! I just got this room cleaned up!"—to his doll later in the day. Not only does his pretend scenario help him understand your perspective and develop his capacity for empathy, it gives him a sense of control that he lacks in the real-life version of things, which can boost his self-esteem and give him a renewed sense of self-confidence. Children enact everything from the mundane to the profound as they attempt to grapple with the issues of their age and stage. Younger preschoolers are likely to be caught up in family dramas about growing up or remaining a baby, while older preschoolers begin tackling scenarios from the world at large, taking on the roles of police officers, firemen, nurses, doctors, retail clerks, and larger-than-life characters like superheroes.

Socially. Pretend play works to enhance children's social development in two ways. First, as two or more children work through a make-believe scenario, they are forced to use the rudimentary social skills they've acquired thus far—sharing, taking turns, coop-erating, compromising, and working out conflicts. Listen to your child as he plays with a friend. You're likely to hear a classic example of cooperative brainstorming: "Let's pretend we're in the circus." "Yeah! I'm the lion tamer and you're the clown." "No! I want to be the lion tamer." "Okay, we're two lion tamers!" The second route to heightened social development is through the actual roles children choose. By acting out the role of judge or teacher, children begin to understand more about how each character is defined in terms of personality, job description, and typical activities.

Intellectually. Language is one of the most obvious areas that your child is exploring during play, because preschoolers still tend, for the most part, to narrate their activities. As your child searches for the right words to describe his toy, he practices vocabulary. As he explains what's happening during his playtime, he works on syntax and structure. And, if he's playing with other children or adults, he stretches his understanding even further by picking up new ways of saying things, new words, new descriptive devices. But language isn't the only thing that expands during play. As your child works out make-believe plots, he brings the hands-on learning of toddlerhood into the symbolic realm. He figures out that a box turned on its side can be a car or a spaceship. He sees that when he gives money to his friend the "cashier" he can "buy" himself a new stuffed animal. As he works with his friends toward a common goal, he begins to understand how to build consensus and use the ideas of others as a jumping-off point for new, creative solutions.

Imaginary friends

Your child may, at one point or another, introduce you to a new friend, and, just when you're wondering where and when he met this person, it will dawn on you: the "friend" is a figment of his imagination. Before you worry whether your child is normal, understand this: Most experts believe it's not only perfectly normal, but maybe even quite healthy, to have an imaginary playmate at this stage of development. It's almost never a sign that he's lonely or upset about something in his life.

Think about it this way: It's a highly creative act to invent an entirely new person out of thin air. There are plenty of adults— authors of fiction and screenplays come to mind—who would give their eyeteeth to be able to quickly and easily devise new characters! Not only is it a sign of strong creativity, but your child's friend may actually foster healthy emotional development and coping mechanisms. An imaginary friend can serve many of the same critical functions as imaginary play. Your child can rehearse real-life scenarios with his playmate—"You must clean up your room," or "Chew your food carefully!"—or use him as a foil for working out his own emotional crises—"Don't worry. That dog won't bite you. He's friendly!" By creating an alter ego whom he takes care of, your child can boost his self-esteem and make himself feel more secure in a wide range of situations.

If you feel your child's imaginary companion is taking up too much of his time or infringing on the family's activities—if he insists that his invisible pal be included in every game—it's time to set limits on their "interaction." Set up a few play dates with real, flesh-and-blood friends, and place gentle limits on when his imaginary friend is allowed to participate—"He can join us at the dinner table," for instance, "but he can't play games with us."

Your child will probably give up his mythical mate soon enough—most children don't carry on with a single imaginary friend for more than about six months—but, in the meantime, you may actually be able to put his fictional friend to good use, appealing to him when your child refuses to get dressed, for instance, or doesn't want to go to school. If you embrace this creature of your child's own creation, you may find him an invaluable ally in dealing with your sometimes-obstinate preschooler.

Distinguishing fantasy from reality

Once your child plunges into the alternative universe of his imagination, you may find it difficult to pull him out again, particularly because many three-year-olds haven't quite sorted out the difference between fantasy and reality. He'll spend a whole day pretending he's a dog and may even insist on being addressed as one for a day or two. Fear not. It's common for kids this age to struggle with questions about reality and fantasy, and there's no need to force him to see the difference just yet.

Being aware of the fact that he isn't totally clear on the difference between pretend situations and real ones can help you avoid common pitfalls of this stage. For instance, something as simple and seemingly innocuous as going to the movies can still be overwhelming for your child, because of the noise, the dark, and the larger-than-life images. If you try a movie date with your child, be prepared to bail out. There's no need to rush it. Put if off for another three to six months or until he mentions a desire to go. At some point soon, he'll hear friends talking about having seen the latest blockbuster, and he'll overcome his fear enough to see what all the fuss is about.

You'll need to monitor what your child sees on the small screen as well. Frightening television shows with scary dinosaurs or monsters, lots of fighting, or even dramatic tension, can strike true terror in the hearts of preschoolers. (Remember, what appears mild to your adult eye may seem much more frightening to a child. When in doubt, skip it.) It's best to save those types of shows for a year or two down the road, when your child is able to watch them without believing that the monster on television could appear in his bedroom at night.

Because your child is so interested in make-believe games, he may ask you to take on the role of goblin or witch while he's playing. You may be tempted to throw yourself into the character with gusto, complete with loud roars or scary cackles. Don't. Your child is more likely to be frightened than entertained by your antics, and you may spend the rest of the day reassuring him that what you did was "just pretend." A better bet: Let your child take on the role of the scary character, and you be the frightened child. Your child will get a kick out of reversing the roles and being the one to hold the reins of power for a while.

Likewise, you need to be careful about threatening to do scary things to him, even in jest. A comment like "I'll throw you out the window if you don't stop whining" might sound to him like a realistic threat. At the very least, it can put a momentary scare in him. At the worst, it can erode his trust in you and leave him feeling anxious for days.

Somewhere between the ages of four and five, your child will begin to be able to distinguish between fantasy and reality with greater ease. You'll see it happening gradually. One day, he'll pretend he's Pinocchio during play, but once he's sitting at the dinner table, he'll say, "Now I'm back to being just me." Even so, if he has a nightmare or sees or hears a scary story, he may need your reassurance that such things aren't real.

Walking through the wonderland together
If you haven't spent much time around children this age, you're in for a real treat. The imagination that blooms during the preschool years will reconnect you with your own creative side and help you see the world in fresh, magical ways. Once your child starts creating pretend scenarios, however, you're going to be in new territory yet again. (Isn't that the never-ending story of parenthood?) Whereas several months ago he wanted you to be a part of all his play activities, he may need more space and privacy just now to explore his own fantasy landscape without your help—or even your presence.

Privacy often becomes an issue at this age. Just as some children want to be left alone to go to the bathroom, many also like to be unsupervised during play. Your child's desire to play alone is actually a good thing. Not only does it indicate a growing sense of independence, but experts believe that solo play gives children's creative impulses the time and space to grow and flourish. It's not difficult to understand why. Just as most adults don't do their best work with someone looking over their shoulder, neither do children feel free to express themselves to the fullest range of their imaginations if they feel the watchful eyes of parents or caregivers.

To cater to your child's need for privacy, make sure he has a small area inside the house that is his designated play area. It doesn't have to be a whole room if space is at a premium. Even a corner of a room, along with a closet or drawer or shelf to keep his things, can be sufficient, as long as it is a space in which your child can play freely, without fear of breaking something valuable or being interrupted.

Participating in your child's play

Sometimes you may want to get involved with your child's playtime. Other times, you'll be relieved that he's willing to leave you out of it. Let your child guide your level of participation. If he asks you to play, join in, but don't try to run the show. Avoid being the know-it-all—"Your tower is going to fall if you build it that high." Instead, do as your child instructs, letting him take the role of the leader in your relationship.

When you do take a more active role, try to make comments that will enhance and enrich your child's play experience. For instance, if your child is the doctor and you are the patient, ask him why you need to take your medicine or why you have to wash off your boo-boos before putting on a bandage. Encouraging him to think about the reasons behind common, everyday activities will get him in the habit of asking questions—and seeking answers.

Understanding your child's love of repetition

You'll see it in every aspect of his life, including language and movement, but it emerges most strongly in play: Your child is at an age when he loves to do things over and over and over again. He'll want to pretend that it's his birthday and you give him a present.

Then he'll want to do it again. And again. In his mind, if it's fun the first time, it will be even more fun the 10th or 20th time. But there's more behind his love of repetition than simply milking a fun activity for all it's worth.

How it feels to be me

I'm not that interested in the toys I used to play with, like the shape sorter and the animal sounds board. Now I love to build huge space-ships that zoom through space or set up fancy tea parties for all my stuffed animals. Lots of times, I don't play with toys at all. I just play in my head, by pretending I'm other people and creatures. Sometimes I play Mommy and Daddy, and I go to the grocery store and tell my friends or dolls what to do. I like to be bossy.

Other times I like to play prince and princess, which makes me feel very special, or Batman and Robin, which makes me feel brave and powerful. It's fun to be the hero and know that I'm strong enough to beat all the bad guys! (I like to shoot them by using a stick as a gun, even though I know you don't like guns.)

I can spend a whole day being somebody else, and it can make me very mad (and a little confused) when you call me by my real name. Can't you see I'm really a cowboy (or a teacher or a construc-tion worker)? I like to play by myself, and I get so caught up in what I'm playing, I often forget where I am. It's like the stuff that's in my head is more real than the things that are actually around me. The great thing I've started to realize is that all my friends like to play the same things I do, and when we get together we make up lots of games that are too hard to explain to anyone else. We spend a lot of time talking about how we're going to fight space aliens or bake a cake and then we spend an even longer time actually doing it. I could spend all day playing—and usually I do!

Repeating things is his way of understanding and learning about them. He's doing the same thing we all do when we're learning about something new—repeating it until he gets it down cold. It's just that, for him, everything is new, so he'll want to repeat things that seem mundane and trivial to you. When he asks you if you want more tea for the zillionth time, try to remember that he's really not trying to drive you around the bend. Going through this ritual is an important way for him to feel capable, confident, and in control.

If your child...	Do say	Don't say
says "I'm not Johnny, I'm Batman!"	"Wow, Batman, you sure are big and strong."	"Batman is just a pretend character. You're a little boy."
won't let anyone sit next to him, because that seat is reserved for his imaginary friend, Gongi	"Gongi is taking a nap right now, but he'll come out to play with you later."	"Gongi isn't real, and I wish you'd stop talking about him."
turns everything from a spoon to a stick into a weapon	"It feels good to get the bad guys, doesn't it?"	"Guns are bad, and I forbid you to even pretend you're playing with one."

HELPING YOUR CHILD GROW
Fostering creativity

Creativity is one of the most prized attributes in our society, and it's one that most of us want our children to hang on to. When your child is in the highly creative preschool stage, you may wish you could freeze his mind just as it is, so he could continue to see the world in such fresh, interesting ways. One of the best ways to encourage his creative tendencies is to indulge them every chance you get. Here are some things to keep in mind to help nurture your child's imagination:

Choose toys that enhance creative development. Toys that can be used as more than one thing are the best choice for children this age. You should have a good supply of paints, markers, crayons, colored pencils, paper, clay, glue, cardboard, and tape. The more resources you have on hand and the more accessible you make them in your house, the more your child is likely to use them and explore the visual aspect of his creativity. Coloring books are fine toys, too, so long as you don't place too much emphasis on staying within the lines and making the pictures look perfect. Other good toys are blocks, dolls, dress-up clothes, flashlights, and big cardboard boxes. You may not see the potential in a cast-off computer box, but your child is likely to see a house, or a spaceship or a fort or a tent. By giving him toys with unlimited possibilities, you give his imagination fertile territory in which to flourish. When choosing toys, pay attention to your child's interests. Some children like to role-play, in which case dress-up clothes or even store-bought costumes will be his dream come true. Others are more interested in visual expression, so having a wide variety of art supplies is important. Still others will be drawn to music, so having a steady supply of new sound-making devices can stimulate and enhance his musical appreciation.

Encourage him to make his own toys. Most parents aren't crazy about the idea of their children turning everything into a weapon. But if you think about it from a creative perspective, using a stick as a sword or a baseball bat as a gun is actually a highly imaginative act. Rather than stifle these efforts, praise the thought that goes into them and urge your child to apply that same type of thinking in other areas. If he sees a character T-shirt he wants on television, for instance, you could encourage him to make his own by buying him a white T-shirt and letting him draw his own picture on it, or by cutting out a picture of his favorite character from a magazine and taping it to the front of a shirt he already owns. He'll see that there are actually a number of ways to get what he wants, some of which are right at his fingertips.

Don't worry about messes. It's easy to get caught up in concerns over household cleanliness. Let's face it: Children this age can wreak havoc on a room. But it's important to not let your desire for cleanliness and order override your child's need for self-expression. Let him take the cushions off the couch to make islands on the floor or create an igloo out of blocks in the middle of his room. Creativity is often a chaotic enterprise. By letting him become immersed in the disorder, you're giving his mind free reign to explore. Don't forget to have him help you clean up. It's just as important for your child to know that there are rules and limits—and playing with toys means picking them up later. You can make the cleanup effort easier for both you and your child by creating clear-cut areas for different categories of toys. Plastic bins or baskets come in very handy for this use. If your child can clearly see that dinosaurs go in one basket and cars go in another, it's easy for him to pitch in and help.

Praise his creative efforts. At this age, it's easy to see what your child is proud of. He'll want to show you the house he's built or the bunny he drew. It can be difficult to stop what you're doing and direct your attention to each and every product of your child's imagination. But by trying to give him a few moments of your undivided attention and commenting thoughtfully on his creative efforts, you'll show him that his work is valuable and important.

Don't let him watch too much TV. Your child is at an age when he's going to become more aware of the television and quite attached to certain programs. There's probably nothing wrong with letting a preschooler watch a little TV—up to an hour a day.

But it's important to set limits on viewing. Allowing your child to sit passively for hours isn't good for him physically or creatively. Educational programs like *Sesame Street* are the most obvious examples of "good TV," but other nonviolent fantasy shows can stimulate your child to "become" new characters and create new play scenarios for himself. Taking an active role in your child's TV viewing can help him get the most out of the experience. Try to watch with him and discuss the program afterward. Some research has shown that when an adult talks to a child about fantasy shows, the child's subsequent play is more imaginative than if he'd watched the show alone.

Resources to foster creativity

For parents:
- *Child's Play: 200 Instant Crafts and Activities for Preschoolers* by Leslie Hamilton (Crown Publishing)
- *Magic Trees of the Mind: How to Nurture Your Child's Intelligence, Creativity, and Healthy Emotions from Birth through Adolescence* by Marian Diamond and Janet L. Hopson (Penguin USA)
- *Your Child at Play: Three to Five Years* by Marilyn Segal, Ph.D. (Newmarket Press)

For children:
- *Harold and the Purple Crayon* by Crockett Johnson (HarperCollins)
- *The Incredible Painting of Felix Clousseau* by Jon Agee (Sunburst)

Software:
- *Magic Artist Studio* (Disney Interactive). This program lets children explore their visual creativity by painting with everything from chalk and markers to an electric toothbrush.
- *Sesame Street: Create & Draw on Elmo's World* (Mattel Media). Preschoolers can create, color, and animate their own art using this fun, clever program.

That scares me!

Your three- to four-year-old's fears

In many ways, your child will seem much older this year, both physically and cognitively. Some days, it would be easy to forget how young she really is if it weren't for one thing: her still-untamed emotions. Although she's made lots of strides emotionally—she can actually calm herself down fairly effectively, for instance, and she can (usually) use words rather than her fists to make her point—you'll be reminded frequently of the fact that she really is closer to babyhood than adulthood when you run up against her fears. And she may have lots of them all of a sudden. (Even a formerly fearless child is likely to become apprehensive during the phobia-prone preschool age.)

Everything from bugs to shadows may give her a fright as she navigates her daily existence.

As a parent, you may find your child's fears confusing. It wouldn't surprise you if a one-year-old screamed in terror when she encountered a dog for the very first time. But it may seem completely baffling when your four-year-old, who was raised with the family Labrador, suddenly retreats behind your leg when a tiny terrier tries to sniff her hand. Preschoolers' fearful behavior is especially bewildering, because so much of the time they're full of bluff and bluster, shouting, "Watch me jump off this step!" "See how I put my shirt on?" or "Look! I wrote my own name." Where does this intrepid individual go when the timid one emerges? The truth is, they're both fighting for space in your little one's psyche. High on all the things she can do one minute, the next she may be terrified by the vastness of the universe, the scale of which she's just starting to comprehend. If there's one thing that's consistent at this age, it's children's inconsistency. So, try to set aside your own notions of what's frightening, and let your child tell you what scares her. Then, do your best to provide comfort and reassurance. Soon enough, she'll put some of the more outlandish, unfounded fears behind her (that the bathroom is scary, even during broad daylight, for instance) and a stronger, more self-assured little person will begin to emerge—just in time for her to wander even farther from the safety of the nest and into the more challenging realm of school.

DEVELOPMENTAL MILESTONE
Gaining a greater understanding of the size and complexity of the world

Watching your child awaken to the limitless variety of people, places, and things in the world is a 90 percent joyful experience. There's nothing like the genuine delight of a child to dust off your attitude and help you see life as magical again. But as she begins to grapple with the vastness of everything, she'll also start to see how small she is—and even you are—in the grand scope of things. There are so many people she doesn't know, so many places she's never been. When you're going somewhere new, she may get quite anxious, especially if you're having trouble finding the exact address. "Are we lost?" she may ask in a panicked voice. Without the perspective and experience of a grown-up, who understands street signs and recognizes landmarks, a young child may find the world dreadfully immense and formidable, a place in which it would be very easy indeed to become hopelessly lost.

Whereas a toddler is aware only of the things she encounters directly in time and space—her family, her house, the grocery store, the baby-sitter—a preschooler has the intellectual ability to see beyond the confines of her existence into the great unknown. She knows that she sees her teacher at school, but she also realizes that her teacher has a life outside of school, with a home and family of her own. Her ability to think about things she can't see brings her face to face with a wide variety of possibilities, some of which are scary. For instance, she may realize that, although you do a good job of protecting her when you're with her, you can't be everywhere at once. You drop her off at school or leave her at home with a baby-sitter. You may even walk out of sight in a department store or let her play in the backyard by herself. The realization that you aren't always there to keep her safe is likely to make her feel quite insecure until she begins to understand that she can rely on other trusted caregivers for help and support.

Your child also is becoming aware of the concept of danger. Not only has she heard you say that certain things are dangerous, she's seen hazardous things happen, both in person and on TV. She's watched adults react in horror when they hear about car accidents or plane crashes, even though she may not fully comprehend the impact of the situation. While your preschooler knows there are many things to be scared of, she doesn't yet know which things truly pose a threat, so she may go through phases in which she's afraid of any number of objects, places, and events that, from an adult perspective, are perfectly harmless. Some of her fears will be useful in keeping her safe as she begins to venture farther afield on her own. (For instance, she may be afraid of cars whizzing by on the street—a fear that could keep her from chasing a ball into the road.) Others are simply stumbling blocks to greater independence that you'll have to help her gradually overcome. Here are some common items on preschoolers' things-I'm-scared-of lists:

The dark. Number one on most kids' list, the dark holds untold fears for preschoolers—for good reason. Young children's imaginations have taken flight, and, in the dark of night, it's easy to let those fertile imaginations run wild. Every noise, shadow, and shape can take on sinister proportions for a small child alone in a big bed. Suddenly, witches creep in the corner of the room, a chair is transformed into a goblin, the murmur of the wind is the sound of bad guys lurking outside.

Young minds are especially vulnerable to fear of the dark when they're tired, which, of course, happens to coincide nicely with bedtime. You can almost see the bravado of the day fading with the late-afternoon sun, as your child becomes more sensitive and scare-prone. A regular, comforting bedtime ritual—a bath, say, then reading in bed—can give your child some extra confidence to face the darkness of night. And responding promptly and in a reassuring but matter-of-fact manner to her fears can help ease her through this tricky stage. One word to the wise: Don't invest too much time in looking for monsters under the bed or in the closet, which may actually give credence to your child's theory that they exist. Instead, help her find ways to feel safe at night. Leave on a night-light. Let her take a flashlight to bed or fashion a sword out of aluminum foil and keep it on her bedside table. Such small, creative measures can give your child the confidence she needs to deal with some of her fears herself.

Dreams. During the day, your child will be able to tell you that "dreams aren't real. They're just things that happen in your head." But, in the middle of the night, when she awakens from a nightmare, she may not be nearly as sure. Because children this age are still struggling with the distinction between reality and fantasy, dreams can seem all too real right after they happen.

If your child awakens from a bad dream, try to reorient her in reality by turning on the light. She'll see that she is indeed in her room (not in the witch's dungeon, after all), and that there's nothing scary in sight. Get her a glass of water or a sip of milk, hand her a trusted stuffed animal or doll to snuggle with, and tuck her in again. Don't make a big deal of it, but don't belittle her fear, either. Nightmares are very real to children this age. Although some children may use the "I'm scared" ploy to push back bedtime, a child who awakens terrified in the middle of the night is almost never faking it. If you're having trouble drumming up much sympathy when you're exhausted too, think about how frightening some of your dreams are, even as an adult. Then imagine what it must feel like to awaken from one and not be 100 percent certain that it wasn't real.

Injury. Since a preschooler is capable of seeing herself as a separate individual, she also starts seeing her body in a proprietary way. Along with that sense of ownership comes anxiety about injury, which is heightened by the fact that, by now, she's fallen down enough to know that, well, falling down hurts. She's probably also heard stories about people who hurt themselves in serious ways—who were hit by cars, or who fell down and broke an arm or leg. Such tales, while worrisome to an adult, can be downright terrifying to a child, who doesn't yet understand the circumstances under which such horrific injuries are likely to occur. Given that, it's perfectly natural for her to suffer some anxiety over the possibility of hurting herself. She may become more cautious on the playground or at the park and ask lots of questions about "things that can hurt you" until she begins to have a better grasp of the hows and whys of personal safety. Letting her know that you're watching out for her, too, can go a long way toward alleviating her fears, but don't be surprised if she vacillates between physical boldness and timidity for some time to come.

Blood. A corollary to the injuries-are-scary attitude that crops up at this age is a fear of blood, even a mere drop of it. It's a classic case of a little information being a dangerous thing. Preschoolers know that blood often accompanies catastrophic injuries, so when they see blood on themselves, they panic, assuming they have been wounded in some dire way. They also may worry that their insides will fall out, since they know that blood is usually supposed to stay inside the body. As a result, you can expect that scraped knees and elbows will take on an added drama for the next couple of years, until your child begins to understand that a small amount of blood will scab over and heal quickly. Knowing that she is likely to scream wildly at the sight of blood can save you from panicking and wondering whether every minor bump requires a trip to the emergency room. Just be sure to keep a good supply of bandages on hand. Calming an injured child usually requires covering up the offending blood as quickly and nonchalantly as possible.

Broken things. Fear of injury can be so pervasive in preschoolers that they're actually afraid of anything that's incomplete, including a chipped plate, a legless doll, or even a cut birthday cake or an unfinished puzzle. From a child's perspective, any imperfection can look like a real threat, because preschoolers tend to relate to everything—toys, animals, clothes—in a much more personal way than adults do. It can be particularly upsetting for preschoolers when a favorite stuffed animal or doll becomes injured, because they identify so closely with special toys. To prevent major meltdowns, fix things quickly if you can. If you can't, be understanding and reassuring, and put yourself in your child's shoes: What looks to you like an inanimate object is, to your child, a dear friend.

People who look or act different. Unless you live in a busy urban area with a wide variety of people, your child may be exposed almost exclusively to people of one particular ethnic background or appearance. If she's never seen someone in a wheelchair, for instance, she may respond with anything from quiet curiosity to earsplitting screams. To avoid histrionics (and public humiliation), don't exacerbate the situation by pushing your child to talk to or interact with people with whom she's obviously uncomfortable. Later, though, be sure to discuss individual differences with her. To spark further discussion, it may help to get a book that depicts people of various ethnicities and physical appearances. By explaining that people come in lots of different shapes and sizes, it's usually fairly easy to defuse this type of fear.

Strangers. Sometime over the course of the next two years, your child will begin to realize that there are a lot more people in the world she doesn't know than people she does. And once she realizes that some of these unknown strangers may be bad guys, she may feel anxious and unprotected—even if you're every bit as watchful and diligent as you've been since she was an infant. She may even go through a phase of asking you if every person you see on the street is a stranger. Bear with her. She's just trying to take stock of the situation. Try to balance her burgeoning fear of strangers with a healthy dose of common sense by explaining that most people are very nice and would rather help than hurt you. *(For more suggestions on how to address the issue of strangers with your child, see page 80.)*

Strange animals. By now you've undoubtedly realized that your child identifies closely with animals, especially pets. It's not hard to understand why: they're small, cute creatures that are supposed to do what adults tell them to do. But at this age, children also begin to realize that animals are often unpredictable. Dogs bite. Cats scratch. Lacking an adult's reasoning ability—that dog is wagging its tail so it's friendly—children may go through a phase of being uniformly fearful when they encounter unknown creatures. Help your child through this stage by passing along your wisdom about animals: "Don't approach an animal that doesn't seem to want to be petted." "If a dog growls or a cat hisses, leave it alone." "Always ask an animal's owner if the pet is friendly." Then, show your child how to pet and talk to an animal, and invite her to join in, but don't force the issue. It may help, too, to read books about animals or to go to a pet store to pet puppies or kittens. Getting her used to the feared creatures in small doses rather than pushing her into an interaction is the best way to extinguish the fear.

Arguments—especially between you and your spouse. By this age, many children understand that some parents get divorced. They may have friends whose parents are no longer together or see a television program in which a child lives with only one parent. Even if your child doesn't have any knowledge of divorce, family arguments can cause her great anxiety. This fear seems almost primal in origin, because it kindles in your child a fear of abandonment, of being left alone with no one to love or care for her. As a result, it's particularly important to be sensitive to your child's fears after you and your spouse argue and to talk about arguments afterward to ease her mind. It's not that you can't fight in front of your child. (But you should try to argue in a healthy way, not hurl insults at one another, because you can be sure your child is taking it all in and learning how to fight by watching you.) Be sure to let her see you make up, too, and reassure her that even people who love each other get in arguments sometimes.

CONFLICT
Wanting independence versus protection

This is an age of major confidence swings. Your swaggering, boasting child can be transformed into a shy, frightened creature in a matter of moments. Her behavior is likely to be confusing to you, but imagine what it must feel like to her! She is struggling to stay in control of her emotions, to be big and brave, yet she's constantly bombarded by new information and incidents that make her feel small and scared—the ambulance rushing by, a flash of lightning, even a reprimand from you can crack her fragile shell of self-confidence. One moment she's shrugging off your embrace, the next minute she's cowering in your arms, wishing she was a baby again so she'd be small enough for you to carry around.

Not only is she frightened of things she doesn't understand in the external world, but she may be anxious about her emotions as well. She may worry that thinking bad thoughts about you when she's angry will make them come true, or that her anger will boil over and she'll hit someone instead of using words to explain how she feels. She may fear that, for all her posturing, she's not as big and strong as she claims to be.

Her temperament may dictate how much time she spends in an outgoing, independent state versus a clingy, dependent one. Children who are extroverted will probably have fewer fears in social situations, but they may still be plagued by fears of the dark or of animals. Likewise, shy children may find lots of things to be afraid of at parties or school, but they may feel brave when they're in the comfort of their own homes. By paying attention to your child's weak spots, you can work with her to overcome or compensate for her most persistent fears.

Expect your child to struggle, no matter what her temperament, when change is afoot in the family. A move, a new sibling, strife in your marriage, or a change in your employment status can bring on an onslaught of anxieties in a preschool-age child. That's because she feels vulnerable, and, although she may seem to understand the events that are happening, her grasp is often more tenuous than it appears. Talking with her about what's going on—repeatedly—and giving her plenty of time and space to express herself can help allay her fears. Sometimes you may simply need to listen to your child and assure her that her feelings are normal. Other times you may need to take a more active role, sharing anecdotes about times when you've felt afraid or helping her develop strategies to feel better about the situation. Be patient and comforting. Most of us carry at least a few fears into adulthood. But by helping your child feel safe, loved, and protected, you can give her a solid base from which to confront the things she fears.

How it feels to be me

Most of the time I'm strong and brave. I can climb to the highest part of the jungle gym and swing way up high on the swing. And I love to go out in the backyard and play all by myself. I feel like such a big kid.

Every once in a while I get a little scared, though, like when the fire truck goes by with its siren blaring or I find a spider in the house or I wake up at night and I'm alone in my dark room. I try not to start thinking of bad things that can happen, but I can't help it. What if the fire comes to my house or the spider is poisonous and it bites me or there's a monster hiding behind the curtain in my room?

Usually I feel good when we're around the house, but when we go out and there are lots of people, I can feel a little overwhelmed. I can't believe how many strangers there are in the world, and I wonder which ones are the ones that do bad things. I wish you could tell just by looking. Once, I couldn't find you in a store, and I got really scared. What if I got lost and never found you again? Where would I live and who would take care of me? I try to stick close by your side, but it's hard. There are so many interesting things to look at, it's easy to get distracted.

When I get afraid, I just want you to hold me tight and tell me everything is going to be all right. It helps if I can talk to you about the things that scare me, but there's nothing that makes me feel more safe than snuggling up on your lap. I wish I felt that good all the time!

Managing your own fears

Your child's fears make her quest for independence a two-steps-forward, one-step-back predicament. But your fears, both spoken and unspoken, can provide stumbling blocks for her as well.

Preschoolers are very sensitive to parental input. They read not only your tone of voice but your body language as well. That's partly what helps them navigate unknown situations. Does Mommy look scared or friendly? Does Daddy sound mad or joking? The information you provide simply by being yourself helps her determine how she should behave.

What your child can't possibly understand is that you, too, have certain fears and foibles, particularly when it comes to her safety. Your fears can send powerful messages about the world to your child. When you meet a big dog on the street, if you shrink away in fear, your child will quickly come to the conclusion that dogs are fierce, frightening creatures. Even Mommy is afraid! When you allow your child to walk across a balance beam but keep saying "Don't fall," your child will hear your underlying attitude—"That's an unsafe thing to do"—loud and clear.

Fearing for your child's safety is a perfectly natural, healthy response to parenthood. It's what makes you insist on holding her hand every time she crosses the street or persist in putting her in a car seat even though she hates it. But it's easy to let your own fears spin out of control and impede your child's progress as an autonomous individual. To maintain a reasonable approach to safety and caution without going overboard, take a good look at the things you're afraid of. Some may be perfectly reasonable. If you have been scratched by a cat, for instance, you might struggle with a fear of cats. But do you want to pass along that fear to your child? If not, you need to take steps to avoid it. Explain to your child what happened to you and why you're afraid of cats, but go out of your way to show her that most cats are harmless by allowing her to pet a friend's or neighbor's cat that you know is friendly.

Likewise, it's easy to react too strongly the opposite way, pushing your child into situations she's not ready for or dismissing her concerns as "silly." If you're feeling impatient with your child's apprehension, it's important to consider why it bothers you. Maybe you don't want her to be saddled with the same fears that plague you. Or perhaps you're feeling competitive with other parents and want your child to be the real go-getter. Either way, you need to back off and give her room to experience what she's feeling. It may help to know that legitimizing her fears, even if they make you uncomfortable, is the best way to help her begin to overcome them.

Inevitably, your child will inherit some of your attitudes. But if you approach each situation with an awareness of what you're bringing to the table, you can do your best to give your child the push she needs toward independence as well as the caring and nurturing she still needs as a small child.

HELPING YOUR CHILD GROW
Overcoming fears

Getting your child past this fearful stage takes time and patience. Hang in there! It can help to know that her fearfulness stems both from her age and inexperience as well as her stage of cognitive development. She understands just enough about the world to be afraid of lots of things, but not enough about it to determine how to deal with or dispel her fears.

That's where you come in. Although you should never push your child to "get over it, already," you can ease her toward quenching some of her fears by taking the following steps:

Be strong in frightening situations. Modeling how to behave is one of the best ways to teach your child. Of course, that's easier said than done when you're in a scary situation, like during a violent electrical storm or on a turbulent airplane ride. To alleviate your child's anxiety, try your best to make eye contact, speak in a calm voice, smile, and remain as matter-of-fact as possible.

Explore the root of your child's fear. Some fears may seem to come out of nowhere. Others stem from an obvious cause. If your child suddenly becomes afraid of the dark after you move to a new house, you can bet the two are related. If the source of your child's fear is obvious, talk to her about it. Reassure her that her new room will soon feel as comfortable as her old one, and, in the meantime, let her think of ways to make it seem as friendly and familiar as possible. Oftentimes, there will be no discernible cause of your child's fears, in which case you need to be comforting and sympathetic, and try not to worry. Fears are a normal part of childhood.

Talk about other people's fears, including your own. Children are often comforted by the idea that they're not the only ones who feel afraid sometimes. There are lots of good children's books that talk about typical childhood fears *(see page 80),* and reading them can give your child an opportunity to discuss the things she's afraid of. Sharing some of your own fears as well as how you try to overcome them can give your child some perspective, by showing her that even grown-ups struggle with anxiety.

Arm her with fear-fighting tools. Children can keep their fears in check with a number of creative strategies that put their vivid imaginations to positive use. For instance, if your child is afraid of the dark, you could ask her what would help her feel safe while she sleeps. Children can come up with extremely effective strategies, from holding on to a stuffed gorilla to wearing superhero pajamas, so they feel strong and powerful.

Use play as a way to help her face her fears. When your child is afraid of something specific, like snakes or spiders, it can be helpful to get toy replicas of the creatures that she can play with. Sit with her and act out scenarios of her choosing. She may want to have the scary creatures do the thing she fears most, like bite her. Don't be alarmed. By pretending the dreaded event has occurred, she actually is becoming less afraid. Or she may want them to be friendly and help her fight other bad guys. Likewise, if she's afraid of a particular situation, such as going to the dentist, you can role play with her, allowing her to take a flashlight and examine your teeth, then exchanging roles. By playacting, you're giving your child the opportunity to examine and explore her fears and become more comfortable with the very things she finds frightening.

If your child...	Do say	Don't say
thinks a shirt in her closet looks like a ghost	"You're right, it does a little bit. But see—it's just your white shirt."	"Don't be ridiculous. It's just your white shirt."
wants her pacifier (or blankie or teddy)	"Okay. You can have it now, but when we go out to dinner I want you to leave it at home."	"It's time for you to grow up and quit being such a baby!"
says that the clown doll she got for her birthday is scary	"Really? What scares you about it?"	"That's not scary It's just a silly old doll."
asks if you're afraid of lions	"Sure, I'd be afraid if I met a lion in the woods, but that's not likely to happen around here. I'm not afraid when I see one in the zoo, because I know it can't get out of its pen."	"Nah. I'm not afraid of anything."

Books dealing with childhood fears

- *Monsters Under the Bed and Other Childhood Fears: Helping Your Child Overcome Anxieties, Fears, and Phobias* by Stephen W. Garber, Ph.D. (Villard)
- *The Preschool Years: Family Strategies That Work—From Experts and Parents* by Ellen Galinksky and Judy David (Ballantine)
- *Solve Your Child's Sleep Problems* by Richard Ferber, M.D. (Simon and Schuster)
- *When I'm Afraid* by Jane Aaron (Golden Books)
- *Your Baby and Your Child: From Birth to Age Five* by Penelope Leach (Knopf)

Raising a safety-conscious child

Although you can't expect a preschooler to be responsible for her own safety, she is old enough to understand some basic concepts about personal safety. When you see her doing something unsafe— running with a pencil, say, or carrying scissors with the blades facing toward her—explain how dangerous it is and tell her why. With simple explanations, children this age can grasp many key issues. Because many of her fears at this age stem from her new understanding of how big the world is, you can help her feel more confident outside the home by teaching her the following simple safety tips:

Stranger dangers. Because the subject of strangers is so interesting to your child, now is a good time to talk about safety around strangers. Although many parents stick with the traditional "Never talk to strangers" rule, this can be quite confusing for a child this age. For instance, you might encourage her to talk to a checker in a grocery store or a waitress at a restaurant, even though they are strangers. A better approach: Direct your advice at bottom-line safety issues—"Never get in a car or go someplace with someone you don't know, even if they say they have a gift or candy for you."

What to do if she gets lost. When you're going to a crowded public place, whether it's a county fair or a shopping mall, point out to your child the people she should turn to if she becomes separated from you. Show her uniformed police officers, museum guards, park attendants, and other officials, and explain to her that those are the people who can help her if she can't find you. Also, explain to her that if she loses sight of you, she should stay in one place, not run around looking for you, since you'll be able to find her more easily if she remains where she was when you saw her last.

Security objects. Most parents realize that it's not uncommon for toddlers to have security objects, but they may expect their preschoolers to be beyond such needs. Often, that's not the case, however. Pacifiers, teddy bears, and favorite blankets may still play a key role in your child's life, and it's a good idea to let her continue to have her cherished object as long as she feels she needs it. Although you may be concerned that her reliance on a security object is a sign of insecurity, it's actually just the opposite. Special toys are a sign that your child has learned to cope with and calm herself in stressful situations without relying on you for comfort.

As your child nears school age, she'll gradually begin to give up her security object on her own. If she doesn't show signs of loosening her grip, you can place limits on when and where she can use the object. For instance, you could say she can have her blanket or pacifier at night, so she feels secure in the dark, but not during the day.

If your child seems overly dependent on a blanket or doll, you should try to get at the source of her neediness. Is she under a lot of stress or anxious about something? If so, you should address the source of her discomfort before insisting that she give up the object that's helping her through it.

The vast majority of children relegate their beloved objects to a shelf once they feel more confident and engaged in life outside their homes. And the peer pressure of school is a sure way to give reluctant children the nudge they need to move beyond their security objects.

Talking to children about death

Until age five, most children are not able to grasp the permanence of death. (It can even be difficult for adults to grapple with the fact that someone they cared about is gone forever.) If your child's grandfather dies, for instance, she may ask repeatedly when he is coming back. Try to be patient with her lack of understanding and explain to her as gently as possible that Grandpa is never coming back.

Whether someone she knows has died or not, your child may develop a real curiosity about death at this age. She may ask over and over when you are going to die and if she, too, will die someday. Answer her questions directly and honestly. For instance, you could say that most people live a long time and don't die until they are very old.

Questions about why and how people die and what happens after they die are best answered as simply as possible. Avoid comparing death to sleep, which can make your child extremely fearful about closing her eyes at night (as can the simple prayer that contains the line "If I should die before I wake"). Instead, you could tell her that people's bodies simply wear out, like batteries in a toy, after they've been used for a very long time. As for questions about what happens after someone dies, you should let your own beliefs guide your explanation. If you believe in God, tell her about heaven. If you don't, explain to her that people's spirits stay with us because we remember them.

With preschoolers, it's best not to go into long explanations of what happens to bodies after they die. Images of being buried in a box or burned may be too frightening for little minds to handle. Instead, reassure her that death is a normal part of life and that, while it may make her sad to lose someone she cares about, it's nothing to fear.

I have friends!

Your three- to four-year-old's ability to socialize

Even with play groups and park dates, parenting a toddler is a relatively solitary pursuit. You hope your child will play with the neighbors' kids, but it never really seems to happen. He plays alongside the other children (experts call this parallel play), but he still does his own thing most of the time, whether he's building with blocks or pushing a baby carriage. When he does try to interact with his peers, he requires lots of intervention from you, because his ability to negotiate the tricky territory of sharing and taking turns hasn't developed yet. More often, he may seem somewhat oblivious to the fact that there are even other children nearby if he's involved in his own game.

Well, all that's about to change. Over the course of the next year, your child will undergo a dramatic shift in the way he interacts with friends. He'll be hungry for companions his own age in a way he's never been before, and he'll likely find his age-mates utterly fascinating (they may even eclipse you in his esteem!). He'll actually relate to his friends in a much more grown-up way, giving you the opportunity to back off and watch their play from the sidelines. He'll relish spending time with favorite friends and exult in the fact that he is capable of having people of his own choosing become part of his life.

Along with the highs of new friendships, however, come the inevitable lows—the moments of being excluded from a game or ostracized at the park. Prepare yourself: If you thought it was difficult to endure childhood hurts when you were the one on the receiving end, wait until your child comes to you with bruised feelings. You'll feel his pain (and then some!), and you'll want to lash out against the perpetrators of his anguish. In fact, keeping your calm so that you can help him negotiate the fickle moods and unpredictable whims of playmates will be one of your most difficult challenges, not only during the preschool years, but for a long time to come.

DEVELOPMENTAL MILESTONE
Learning to play cooperatively

The dawn of the preschool era brings with it the awakening of a whole new set of social skills in your child. The most important of these, the one that will help him make the transition from parallel play to interactive play with peers, is the ability to cooperate during social get-togethers.

In order to make this leap, your child will begin to shed some of his former selfishness (characterized by grabbing toys, hitting, lashing out, or screaming "That's mine!"). He'll also learn to contain his emotions for the greater good of a group enterprise, whether it's building a castle out of blocks or playing a game of house. His new awareness of boundaries won't happen overnight. But if you watch closely, you'll see gradual changes as your child evolves into a more social being—by sharing toys without a fuss, handling disagreements with the aplomb of a diplomat, and actively participating in group games that involve a hefty dose of imagination.

Learning to share. Your child's first steps toward sharing will be tentative. Instead of allowing another child to have his toy, he may try to find a similar toy for his friend or even a different type of toy the other child would like instead. It might not look like much, but this is unmistakable progress. Several months ago, he would have cared only about protecting his precious things. Now, he understands that other children have needs also—and he wants to help them fulfill those desires.

Further evidence of his newfound sharing skills will come when your child accepts another child's claim on a toy—"That's my doll!"—without getting into a tussle. Make no mistake: There will still be plenty of fights over toys. Most three-year-olds still view their belongings as an extension of themselves. As a result, letting a friend play with a toy is tantamount in your child's mind to giving away his arm or leg! He also may not quite grasp the difference between a temporary loan and a permanent gift, so he'll continue to be anxious about allowing toys out of his possession for fear he'll never get them back. You'll find that fights over toys will gradually diminish as your child and his peers accept these key concepts.

By the time your child is four, he may be able to share quite easily, although some children still struggle with this until they're about five. Easing the process is your preschooler's fluency with language. He knows that, instead of swiping a toy from another child, he can ask if he can have it. He knows, too, that if someone else wants his toy, it's in his best interest—the interest of maintaining a calm, pleasant play environment—to acquiesce. To an older preschooler, it's often more important to keep an activity going than to squabble over who holds what object in his possession.

Learning to take turns. As your child becomes more adept at sharing, he'll also catch on to the concept of taking turns, which allows a disputed toy to become an object of cooperation rather than confrontation. Not only will he understand that if he waits for a few minutes, he'll get a chance to play, but he will also have the patience (most of the time) to wait his turn.

With younger preschoolers, you may have to be the arbitrator of turn-taking. It can help to set a timer or let your child look at your watch to see how much time he will get. (Even though he can't yet tell time, he'll be comforted by the fact that he has a chance to look at your watch.) If each child gets two or three minutes with the toy, they're usually happy and, after a turn or two, will find something else to play with. Older preschoolers may be able to take turns on their own, handing a toy back and forth without too much difficulty.

Learning to negotiate problems. Young preschoolers may still have difficulty working through problems on their own, so you may need to be on hand to intervene when disputes get heated. Gradually, however, your child and his peers will learn to deal with these tricky issues themselves by parroting the words and strategies they've heard you and other adult caregivers use to settle quarrels. (Keep in mind that their ability to do this will break down if they're not feeling well, they're hungry, or they're tired.) As a result, you may see your child begin to get into a sudden argument, then be able to de-escalate the confrontation by saying "If you get that doll, then I get this one!" and continue to play happily.

Be prepared for volatility, however. Even older preschoolers are prone to lashing out verbally at friends if they feel they've been slighted in some way. You may hear your child say, "I don't want to play with you anymore!" or "You're not my friend!" Often, when things get to this point, your child will ask you for help solving the problem. If he doesn't, take these exclamations as your cue to intervene.

Learning to respond to another's actions. A final key to cooperative play—the one that makes it play rather than simply spending time in tandem—is the ability to respond to things someone else says or does. As your child develops both cognitively and emotionally over the next two years, he'll make great strides in this regard. At first, his attempts at playing imaginary games with other children will be quite stagnant. For instance, young preschoolers may say they're playing house or superheroes, but, apart from assigning the key roles, they won't actually *do* much. Many three-year-olds don't seem to understand yet how to plumb their imaginations to create new play scenarios or how to incorporate the suggestions of others to build a storyline.

By the time your child is four, however, you'll see growth in this skill, to the point where he can get together with a friend or group of friends and create elaborate pretend scenarios that are very fluid, with each child contributing new ideas—"Let's say the kids make a mess in their room and the mom gets mad!" "Yeah! Then the kids clean up the mess and get to eat Popsicles!"—that take the play in new directions.

The increasing importance of friends

Not only will your child become more capable of playing with friends in the next two years, but friends will become increasingly important to him as well. In fact, young preschoolers who haven't quite gotten the hang of playing together may be more interested in watching each other than in participating in any particular activity. You'll see your child eyeing other kids on the playground, noticing his peers' art projects, and watching how they play with their toys or wash their hands.

Gradually, he'll begin to identify with children his own age, and, as he does, he may want to emulate how they talk, dress, or behave. Your child who used to hate hats may suddenly insist on wearing one every day, "because Karl wears one." Or he may develop a sassy attitude like one of his more frequent playmates.

Although you may not welcome all of the various influences of your child's peers, most of the behavior is temporary and not worth worrying too much about. Children this age often change allegiances frequently—a friend one day may be left out the next—and a child who seems to be a "bad influence" may just be going through a brief stage of orneriness, after which he'll return to being a really nice kid.

Even though preschoolers still have frequent fights with friends, their bonds run deep. This is often the age at which best friends begin to pair up, as your child finds someone whose interests and temperament dovetail nicely with his own. He may develop a sense of ownership over his friend and get jealous and upset if his friend plays with (or even talks to) someone else.

The strength of these early friendships may reveal itself in lots of physical affection. Your child and his special friends will throw their arms around each other by way of greeting, give each other kisses, hold hands constantly, and sit next to each other every chance they get. They not only want to reassure each other of their enduring affection, but also let others know that they are a tight-knit pair.

Being excluded or excluding others

The flipside of your child's burgeoning interest in friendship is being excluded, and, although many parents are shocked when it first happens to their preschooler, this is the stage at which it commonly appears. That's because young children seem to define their friends not only by who they like but by who they don't like. Maybe it gives them a sense of power to say no to someone or serves to unify the group they've chosen to play with. In any case, at some point, your child is likely to come to you in tears saying, "They said I couldn't play with them!"

Although leaving someone out simply for the sake of exclusion typically happens more in the younger preschool years, more complicated types of exclusionary behavior begin to erupt as children turn four. Your child may be devastated, for instance, when his best friend decides he wants to branch out and play with other children as well. Or your child may be pursued by someone he isn't interested in playing with. Or your child may be part of a threesome, in which two friends like the third better than they like each other. Such situations may bring back lots of not-so-fond memories of your own childhood and make you feel extremely protective of your own child's emotions. It can help to remind yourself that everyone experiences such unpleasant episodes—and everyone survives them. At this age, it's best to look at painful incidents as learning experiences that can give your child the opportunity to grow emotionally.

CONFLICT
Selfish desires versus social needs

As your child's social universe expands, new demands will be placed on him as a human being. No longer will he be able to cling to toys as if they were a part of himself or hit friends without learning a difficult rule or two: No one likes to play with someone who can't share or who is a bully.

Although developmentally he's just now at an age where he can understand things like sharing and taking turns, his learning curve will be accelerated by his own growing need for friendship and by an age-old force known as peer pressure. You may have told him he needs to share a thousand times, but when the same words come out of the mouth of another pint-size person, they can have the impact of a tidal wave.

As he wades into groups of other children, some of whom will be more socially adept than he is, and some less, he'll be forced to decide: Is it more important to keep my toys to myself or to play with my peers? Young preschoolers may remain firm in their desire to hoard their belongings. But gradually your child's desire to interact with his peers will overwhelm his selfish urges, and he'll be willing to give up a little control for some more group play.

Don't expect a linear progression or an overnight transformation, however. One day your child may be able to share his toys with a friend without so much as a sniffle. The next day he may scream bloody murder the moment another child looks at his stuff. Like everyone, your child has moods that are favorable to playing with peers and moods that will make him simply unfit for human companionship. It will help his progress as a social being if you learn to distinguish between the two and make judgments about when to go on playdates and when to stay home and reschedule.

Obvious things like hunger, fatigue, and illness can impair your child's ability to meet the demands of a social environment. But subtler issues will come into play as well. Your child may be less able to share when he's feeling emotionally vulnerable because of stress at home or a change in his preschool or day care. He may clash with one particular child more than others (a situation that can create difficulty if it happens to be the child of your best friend), or he may behave better around old friends than new ones, especially if he tends to be shy or slow to warm up in new situations. Getting to know your child's own particular quirks can help you recognize when he'll need extra help—and when he's ready to jump into the fray and play like a big kid.

YOU AND YOUR CHILD
Giving your child the freedom to socialize

In so many ways, being the parent of a preschooler requires maintaining a delicate balance between being overprotective and allowing too much independence. Once your child has embarked on his life as a small socialite, you'll find yourself engaged in a subtle variation of that challenge once again. You need to allow your child to make his own way in the world of his peers, but be right there to mediate problems (especially at first), wipe away tears caused by hurt feelings, or give him a hug when he's tired at the end of a long play session.

Typically, younger preschoolers need more adult supervision during play than older preschoolers, because four-year-olds have learned to negotiate many of their own problems more effectively. They can often work out toy disputes or change the direction of play if someone is unhappy with what's going on.

Even so, there will be times when your adult authority is required, so you (or another adult) should never be too far away when your child is playing. He'll still come to you when he runs up against a seemingly insurmountable problem or to tattle on the misbehavior of a friend (a favorite activity at this age): "Matt is playing with the red car but I want it, too, and there's only one," or "Anna hit me!" Your calm, reassuring presence will keep your little one anchored, give him confidence to venture forth, and teach him how to find solutions to every kind of problem.

While you need to be available for your child, your physical presence isn't required every moment he's playing. In fact, having an adult in the room can actually stifle children's play, making them feel inhibited and self-conscious. Better to busy yourself with some project in a nearby room (preferably within earshot), and let your child know where he can find you if he needs you.

Taking a back seat to your child's peers
While it can be a relief to finally leave behind the "hover mode" that comes with being the parent of a toddler, giving your child the freedom to play without a chaperone also can be disconcerting at first, especially for first-time parents who are used to providing constant supervision and have held the title of favored playmate until this point. It's time to get used to this new reality, however. You're no longer the be-all and end-all person in your child's universe.

He not only may prefer playing with his friends, but he also may talk to them more (some studies have found that preschoolers spend more time talking to peers than to adults) and listen to them more. Your child will begin to come home from playdates bursting with important information gleaned from friends: "A carnosaur is a dinosaur that eats meat," or "Rain comes from clouds." Meanwhile, your own interesting tidbits of information seem to fall on deaf ears.

If you're feeling slightly hurt by the change in your relationship, don't take it too hard. First, rest assured that your reaction is normal. You're dealing yet again with that process of letting go, and it's never easy. And you should keep in mind that, while his friends are new and exciting to him, he still relies on you for most things and will continue to do so for some time to come.

Finally, it can help to remind yourself of one of your long-term goals in child rearing—to raise a socially well-adjusted, happy child. One of the best ways to do that is to provide him with plenty of opportunities to play with other children, then give him the space to play (and fight) with his friends on his own terms.

If your child...	Do say	Don't say
says that nobody likes him	"Are you sad because Justin played with someone else today?"	"Don't be silly. Of course they like you!"
says he likes one friend better than another	"It's okay to have a favorite friend, but it's important to be nice to everyone."	"I do, too."
says he can't make friends	"Next time we're at the park, I'll help you go up to someone and tell them your name. Would you like to practice now with your stuffed animals?"	"Everyone knows how to make friends. It's easy!"

How it feels to be me

I love my friends. We like to do all the same things—like splash in puddles, zoom around the playground like airplanes, and have tea parties. I can't believe there are other people who like to do these things as much as I do!

And my friends are funny, too. When we're together I laugh and laugh. Sometimes we act really silly and do crazy moves with our bodies or make funny noises. Other times we say funny words like "poop" and "booger." That just cracks me up, even though I know you don't think it's that funny.

When I wake up in the morning, I usually start thinking about my friends and who I'm going to play with that day. If I have a playdate or get to go to school, I get really excited and jump around the room. I really look forward to the times when I get to be with people my own age.

Blue is my favorite color, because that's the color my best friend likes, and we try to wear something blue every day. One day, he wore green because this other little boy likes green, and I felt like crying all day. I was glad to talk to you about it when I got home, and you were right: By the next day, he was wearing blue again and everything was all better.

Sometimes my friends and I fight and it makes me feel really bad. The older I get, the more I try to do things that they will like so that they won't get mad at me, and usually we get along really well. I'm sad to say good-bye to my friends at the end of the day, but I'm usually pretty tired, too, and once I'm home, I'm glad just to be with you again.

Raising a socially well-adjusted child

Parents want nothing more than to have their children be happy and well liked, to have them be kind to others, to make sure they get along in the social milieu. But inevitably, as they make their way through the gauntlet of friends and schoolmates, there will be hurts and disappointments. A bully will pick on your child. Your child won't be invited to a big birthday party. He'll have fights with friends. And he'll dish it out, too. He'll be mean to other children or rude to adults or aggressive with a sibling. That's because he's a child, navigating in a world full of children, and children don't know any better. It's up to parents to teach them. Here are some ways to offer support, help your child cope with and comprehend the complexities of social relationships, and guide him toward becoming a good friend—to everyone.

Helping him solve conflicts and quarrels. Getting your child to see another person's point of view is critical when it comes to helping him fix the unavoidable rough patches in friendships. By the age of three, your child is becoming more capable of understanding someone else's point of view, although he usually won't be able to see it without your help. If your child is upset because he wants to play with his friend's special toy car, you may be able to give him a lesson in empathy and solve the problem by saying, "You know how you feel about your special teddy bear? You don't like anyone else to play with it, right? Well, that's the way Emily feels about her toy car. It's her special toy that she keeps just for herself."

Other times, you can point out areas of compromise—"If you let Joey have the black Batman, I'll bet he'll let you have the yellow one"—or institute an enforced session of taking turns. Set the timer for two or three minutes to give the first child his turn, supervise the play to be sure there are no attempts at toy stealing in the meantime, then give the disputed toy to the second child for the same amount of time. Most children won't be able to do this on their own until they're at least four (and sometimes five), but you're teaching him little by little the important lesson of give and take.

When physical violence breaks out (which still happens fairly frequently at the preschool age) pull apart the combatants and have a talk with both of them. It's less important to determine who started the melee than to show children how to solve it. Remind them that they must use words instead of their fists and encourage them to apologize to each other, but don't turn that into another battle. If they resist strongly and emotions are still running high, give them both a cooling-off time-out. If one child has a visible scratch or red spot, point it out to the other child and appeal to his empathy: "Look at Kathy's arm. That must hurt, don't you think? It's not okay to hurt your friends."

If a playdate continually gets out of hand, give the children a warning—"If you two can't get along, Jeremy is going to have to go home"—then follow through if things don't improve. It can be difficult to call another parent and send a child home. But the good news is, you'll probably have to be this harsh just once. Appropriately severe consequences tend to get children's attention!

Learning the rules of social relationships requires lots of practice. Keep in mind that your child is a novice. With time, he'll be better able to control himself and master all the skills you're trying to teach him.

Dealing with hurt feelings from being excluded. At this age, there's almost no such thing as a popular child. Every child, at one point or another, is rejected by friends—even best friends. If your child comes home in tears one day saying, "David wouldn't let me play with him," give him your undivided attention. Such declarations are clearly a cry for help, and being there for him when he needs you, rather than being distracted by other things you have to do, will lay the groundwork for a good relationship and future shared feelings.

Listen to what he says, then ask him some gentle questions: "Why didn't he let you play with him? or "Can you explain what happened?" Some children will be better able to do this than others. Whether you get the details or not, let your child know you understand how he feels—"You sound very sad about this"—and acknowledge that being excluded can be very hurtful. It might help to share a personal story about a time when your friends didn't include you in a get-together or didn't invite you to a party to let him see how universal the experience is.

If your child is excluded while you're watching, intervene on his behalf by suggesting a role he could take in whatever play scenario the children are creating. If the situation happens at preschool, point it out to a teacher, who will probably be able to help your child get involved with a group activity.

Sometimes arranging a playdate with one or two children from a particular group can help your child gain a toehold in the social order, but if it's clear that the children don't have much interest in your child, it's better to help him focus his attention on making other friends. It's also important to let him know that there's nothing wrong with him, perhaps by pointing out that he, too, prefers some friends over others.

Helping a shy child make friends. In general, timid children are born, not made. Studies show that, even as infants, shy children are more bothered by things like light and noise than other babies. If your child is slow to adapt to new situations, he is more likely to be shy than children who jump right into new activities. Although there's nothing wrong with being shy, it's important not to label your child that way, or he may believe the label—with no hope of ever being anything else. Being aware of your child's temperament, however, can help you foresee situations in which he might struggle and help him feel more comfortable.

Shy children often make very good friends, because they tend to be loyal and trustworthy, but forming the initial friendships can be difficult, largely because they are usually somewhat behind in developing the social skills it takes to bond with other children. That's where you come in. Give your child some easy opening lines to use when he meets other children: "Hi, my name is Charlie. What's yours?" or "I have my trucks with me. Would you like to play?" or "Can I play, too?" It can help to practice these statements at home, either between the two of you or by playacting the scenarios with stuffed animals.

Set up playdates with other children, particularly those who seem temperamentally suited to your own child. (A particularly gregarious child can be overwhelming to one who's on the shy side.) It can help to invite the child to your house, if your own child feels most comfortable on his own turf.

Prepare your child in advance for big social events, like parties and group outings. Tell him who will be there and what will happen, so he knows what to expect. Then, don't force your child to dive into the social mix at parties, but allow him to hang back until he feels comfortable. Given the freedom to interact at his own pace, he'll enjoy himself and gain the necessary confidence to venture forth a little more quickly next time.

Interacting with siblings. While your child makes friends in the wider world, he may also have a built-in comrade at home in the form of a sister or brother. If the two are close in age, they will start to spend more time playing together at this point. But they'll also spend what may seem like unbelievable amounts of time engaged in battles over everything from who gets the first cupcake to whose turn it is to shut off the television.

Keep in mind that your child has different issues with his siblings than he does with his friends, the most important of which is that he has to share your love and affection with his brother or sister. That basic struggle is often at the heart of sibling conflicts.

To avoid constant upheaval, try to spend time with each child alone, to let them know that you love them both. Take a look at the time of day or specific situations that typically cause problems and avoid them whenever possible. For many children, the period right before dinnertime is a particularly difficult time. If it's possible, try to separate your children during this time of day; if it's not, give them each some crayons and paper for coloring, read them a book, or let them watch a video or short television program. Keeping the activity quiet and low-key can go a long way toward making it through the "witching hour" unscathed.

Usually, preschoolers are fairly good with baby siblings, especially if you appeal to their egos and let them be your (invaluable!) assistant in dealing with the infant. Even so, there will be times when resentment and jealousy rear their ugly heads. Keep a watchful eye on your child's mood. If he's tired or cranky, try to give him some extra love and attention and make sure he's engaged in his own activities when you tend to the baby.

Books about relating

For parents:
- *Beyond Sibling Rivalry: How to Help Your Children Become Cooperative, Caring, and Compassionate* by Peter Goldenthal, Ph.D. (Owl Books)
- *Nurturing Good Children Now* by Ron Taffel, Ph.D. (Golden Books)
- *The Shy Child: Helping Children Triumph Over Shyness* by Ward K. Swallow, Ph.D. (Warner Books)
- *The Shy Child: A Parent's Guide to Preventing and Overcoming Shyness from Infancy to Adulthood* by Philip G. Zimbardo and Shirley L. Radl (ISHK Book Service)

For children:
- *George and Martha: The Complete Stories of Two Best Friends* by James Marshall and Maurice Sendak (Houghton Mifflin)
- *I'm a Big Brother* by Joanna Cole (William Morrow & Company)
- *The Rainbow Fish* by Marcus Pfister (North South Books)

Helping children interact with adults. As your child's social realm expands, it can include not only peers, but other parents, teachers, and casual adult acquaintances. Helping your child learn to interact with adults can be almost as important as helping him interact with peers, because it teaches him to be comfortable with a variety of people and use his social skills in a number of different settings.

Talking to your spouse and including your child in family discussions can help your child see how to participate in a conversation. Encourage your child to participate by asking him questions, but place limits on his talking if he tries to dominate family dialogue. Remind him that interrupting isn't polite. He must wait his turn to talk, just as Mommy and Daddy do, and he should try to listen to what others say as well.

Preschoolers are not too young to learn simple skills, like making eye contact when they speak with someone and responding when an adult asks them a question. Let your child practice these social graces as you make your way through your daily errands. Show him how to be friendly to people you see along the way, and encourage him speak to the butcher or the dry cleaner, let him place his own order at restaurants, and give him the opportunity to talk on the phone when Grandma calls. When someone asks him a question and he doesn't respond, gently remind him to be polite by getting down to his level and repeating the question.

Encourage your child to talk to his teacher at school by suggesting that he tell her about a special weekend activity. It's too much to expect your preschooler to have the social finesse of an adult. But, with practice, he can learn to be polite and have conversations with people of all ages.

I'm the best!

Your three- to four-year-old's personality

Like adults, children exhibit a wide range of personalities. By the time they're preschoolers, traits like shyness, extroversion, patience, high energy, compassion, sensitivity, and distractibility begin to emerge. You'll see bits of yourself in your child—you'll realize she inherited not only your blue eyes but also your tendency to withdraw in crowds—and you'll watch with amazement as your child exhibits characteristics that are completely foreign to you. Maybe she'll be able to spend hours putting together puzzles or have a quirky sense of humor or reveal a contagious enthusiasm when she gets interested in a game or activity. All these characteristics are part of her inborn temperament, the genetic hand she was dealt at birth.

If your child has certain unpleasant traits, don't worry: Her personality isn't fixed for life by the time she reaches three or four. Young children are still developmentally immature, and their personalities will change as they become more aware of the world around them. In addition, life experiences will shape who your child becomes as much as will her inborn tendencies. She'll learn that being aggressive can make playmates angry or that being too timid causes her to be overlooked. Still, as your child becomes increasingly verbal and interacts more with the world, you'll see certain innate biases begin to reveal themselves, and paying attention to them will help you be a better parent.

If your child has a lot of energy, for instance, you can avoid confrontations by staying away from situations that require long periods of quiet inactivity—graduation ceremonies, movies, even church. A shy child may need lots of support and encouragement when she's venturing into new territory—especially preschool, where the children, teacher, and classroom may all be foreign to her. A child who is easily frustrated will need you to guide her away from potentially explosive situations (when she is trying to master a new, somewhat difficult task, like tying her shoes for instance) and will need your help to learn to harness her patience.

Getting to know your child as a person requires not only keen observation but also a certain objectivity, which can be difficult. As parents, we all want our children to be perfect. It can be tough to admit that your child is emotionally intense and hard to manage, for instance, or that she has trouble sticking with a project, partly because you may feel it reveals some basic inadequacy in your ability as a parent. But it's important to realize that you didn't consciously create your child's temperament any more than you chose her hair color.

Moreover, you need to keep in mind that traits that seem

unpleasant at age three might be real assets as your child ages. A high-energy, extroverted child may be exhausting for a parent—who has to chase her around—but a high-energy, extroverted adult might excel as an actor, a career that requires long hours and a love of the limelight. Taking the long view can help you see your child's personality not as strictly positive or negative but as a set of traits that can be better or worse depending on the situation. Most important, the more clearly you understand what makes her tick, the better able you'll be to help her learn and grow and, as she matures, help her gain some understanding of her own temperament. By doing so, you'll provide her with an invaluable gift: self-awareness.

DEVELOPMENTAL MILESTONE
Developing inflated self-confidence

While preschool children are as different as leaves on a tree, they have certain common characteristics that typically come to the fore during this stage. One of the most prevalent is a certain swaggering, boastful self-confidence. Listen in on your child's conversations with friends, and you're likely to hear a one-upmanship contest: "I can run really fast." "Yeah? Well I can run even faster." "Well I'm the fastest runner ever in the whole wide world!"

By the time we're adults, our tendency to boast is tempered by experience. We realize that other people don't like a braggart and that we often are not the smartest, strongest, or fastest person on the block. We learn modesty and self-deprecation, traits that help us fit in and be well liked. As a result, our children's boasting often strikes a negative chord. You may even worry, when you hear her sing her own praises for the umpteenth time, that your child will turn into an unlikable lout.

You can set your mind at ease on that account. The bragging that typically appears at this age is a normal part of development. (How else to explain the fact that nearly every child, from the wallflower to the supersocial, displays the same type of behavior?) Your child has just taken a giant step away from babyhood and feels her

own power more keenly than ever before. Likewise, she's beginning to understand that you are not all-powerful, a realization that
can be exciting even as it's a little scary. And the typical preschooler is simply an exuberant person. She *loves* things or *hates* them;
she never walks if she can run; she laughs and cries with equal
abandon; and she exaggerates almost everything: "That dog was
as big as our car!" "We walked for miles." "My dad is 25 feet tall."

Her love of hyperbole naturally extends to her own abilities.
But there is more to it than that. Your preschooler is truly
impressed with how high she can jump, how well she can express
herself, and how much she understands. And she expects everyone
else to be impressed, too, because, from her perspective, she has no
equal. Although she's beginning to be able to see other people's
points of view, she's still egocentric enough to feel that her drawing,
her ability to swing, and her house are, in reality, the best.

As your child makes her way through the next two years, she'll
begin to shed the shell of her egocentricity. In other words, your
child's top-of-the-world phase is just that—a phase. But it's important to treat it gently and respectfully, because it's during this first
blossoming of self-perception that the seeds of self-esteem are sown.

CONFLICT
Coping with defeat

While your preschooler's self-confidence may be at an all-time high,
it's very fragile, and the more understanding she gains of the world,
the more easily her self-esteem will be shattered by the realization
that she is not actually the best at everything. Her sense of frustration and disappointment may emerge most strongly when she's
struggling to master a new skill, whether it's learning to ride a bike
or figuring out how to assemble a model airplane. Her natural temperament will dictate how many setbacks she can take, but even
the most persistent child will reach her boiling point sometimes.

If your child is struggling with a skill, help her gauge her
progress by pointing out how much she has learned already. For

instance, to a child who's frustrated about trying to color within the lines of a coloring book, you could say, "When you were little you had trouble even holding a crayon, and now look at you!" If she loses at Chutes and Ladders, stave off the "I'm no good at games" mindset by reminding her that her daddy lost last time or that she's won many times at Candyland.

Your child's ego will also take a battering as she makes her way through preschool and social gatherings. There, she's going to run into lots of other people—namely, her peers—who don't think she's the best. In fact, they may think they're better than she is, and indeed, they *will* actually be better at some things.

Expect some conflict as more than one child tries to assert a claim of "I'm the best" on everything from hopscotch to cleanup time. The pecking order will begin to be established naturally, as more aggressive children boast loudest and longest. Mellower preschoolers may be able to find a compromise to their dueling claims of grandeur. "We're both the best," one will say, and they'll both continue to play happily. Other times, you may need to step in and mediate a solution—"You're both very fast runners," or "Both pictures are nice. I like the yellow Julie used in her picture and the green you used in yours."

Your child may be disgruntled at your response. Naturally, she wants you to think she's the best at everything. But she should learn that other children's efforts have merit, too. It's a hard lesson, but if she is given the message lovingly, she'll understand that other people's successes don't have to be her failures, a lesson that will serve her well during the competitive school-age years.

YOU AND YOUR CHILD
Dealing with bragging

Your own natural aversion to bragging may make it difficult for you to listen to your child's boasting. On the other hand, you may secretly enjoy it. How you respond to your child's behavior is dictated by your own temperament. If you tend to be fairly exuberant and self-confident, you may laugh off even your child's most outrageous boasts. If you're more shy and withdrawn, a minor self-congratulatory statement may make you cringe with embarrassment.

Either way, it's important to understand that your temperament is coming into play as you interact with your child and to moderate your response accordingly. Agreeing with your child—"Yes, you were the best one in the play"—isn't the best approach; nor is undermining your child with statements like, "Don't be so boastful. That's not nice!" Better to make note of a praiseworthy quality—"I was proud of the way you sang all the songs"—and leave it at that.

How it feels to be me

When I run, it seems like my legs are moving unbelievably fast. I like to look down and watch them as I go. There couldn't be anyone in the world who runs faster. When I draw a picture, I'm so proud of what the colors look like on the page. It feels like such a big accomplishment. When I eat my soup and don't spill one drop, I feel so happy. Can you believe how good I am at using a spoon?

When I hear someone talking about a child, I often think they're talking about me. It's hard for me to believe that people pay much attention to other kids. I'm so interested in everything I can do that I expect everyone else to be interested, too. It's great when you let me know how proud you are of things I do. I love to show you all my new tricks—over and over and over.

I may get sad or frustrated or angry sometimes. If I lose a game or fall off the monkey bars, I suddenly feel very small, like I'm a real little kid again. Then I need you to comfort me and tell me something that will make me feel better. Usually it doesn't take much, because I have a lot of energy and I like to be happy and on the go. In fact, most of the time I feel really good about being me!

If your child...	Try to	Try not to
is active	Provide opportunities for her to vent her energy and experiment to find out what calms her down.	Force her to sit quietly for long periods of time.
is slow to adapt to new situations	Establish a consistent routine and discuss the day's schedule with her in the morning **or** introduce new things—whether it's food, activities, or toys—in small doses **or** in new social situations, let her venture out at her own pace.	Spontaneously switch activities without giving her warning, expect her to make the transition to bedtime mode easily, or push her to jump into new social situations.
is emotionally intense, loud, and dramatic	Remind yourself that every situation isn't a crisis just because your child is reacting strongly, and experiment to find out what soothes her.	Treat every minor incident as a major disaster or get caught up in her emotional maelstrom, especially if you're an intense person, too.
has irregular bio-logical rhythyms, characterized by out-of-sync eating and sleeping patterns	Have healthy snacks on hand so she can grab food on the go and give her small portions at mealtime **or** experiment with naps and bedtimes to see what suits her best.	Turn mealtime into World War III by expecting her to eat according to the family's schedule.

If your child...	Try to	Try not to
is easily frustrated or bored	Teach her new skills in stages so she doesn't become overwhelmed, and keep lessons short.	Push her to learn new things too quickly or be competitive with other children about acquiring new skills, like learning to tie her shoes.
is physically sensitive	Avoid things that bother her. If she is sensitive to noise and chaos, opt for a small preschool or day-care center. If she's easily irritated by scratchy fabrics or tags, buy soft cotton apparel and cut out the tags. If she's annoyed by minor physical ailments, treat her pain respectfully and give her appropriate doses of over-the-counter pain relievers.	Disregard her complaints (especially if you have a high tolerance for physical discomfort) or chastise her by calling her a "baby" or a "wimp."
is adaptable	Set aside time to talk to her to be sure her needs are being met. An easygoing child can be overlooked, especially if she has a high-needs sibling.	Assume that everything is okay just because she's not complaining.

If your child...	Try to	Try not to
has a low activity level	Choose games and activities—like reading, drawing, and board games—that cater to her love of quiet **or** encourage her to be physical by playing actively with her **or** give her plenty of time to do things, like get dressed for preschool or day care.	Expect her to be enthusiastic for long periods of high-energy play. push her to move more quickly.

Negotiating temperamental conflicts

Every time you interact with your child, both of your temperaments will affect the outcome. Some parents have a natural fit with their children, they seem to "click" without too much conflict, and their strengths and weaknesses are more complementary than clashing. More often, however, there are at least some areas of chafing.

Sometimes you and your child may actually be too much alike for your own good. You're both stubborn, so you tend to butt heads, or you both like to be the center of attention. Other times, you may find it difficult to understand her behavior because it's so different from your own innate response. If you're the gregarious type, you may have trouble giving your shy child time to adjust to new situations, or if you like to see a project through to completion, you may have trouble enjoying your child's company if she tends to be more of a hummingbird, flitting quickly from activity to activity.

As your child enters this new age during which she is blossoming into her own person, it's a good idea to take a few minutes for self-reflection. Ask yourself what your natural response is in different situations. Do you like to be the belle of the ball, or do you prefer to watch from the sidelines? Do you adapt to new situations easily, or does it take you time to adjust? Are you sensitive to things like hot and cold or loud noises, or are you oblivious to your environment? Do you prefer to spend your time on the go, or are you more likely to sit and read a book?

By understanding your own temperament and seeing how it melds with your child's, you can avoid potential areas of conflict, exploit areas of harmony, and seek to put your own personal biases aside as you allow your child to find her own way in the world.

HELPING YOUR CHILD GROW
Building the foundation for healthy self-esteem

People who like themselves tend to be likable people. That's why it's not as important to worry about your child's minor personality quirks at this age as it is to make sure she feels good about herself. To help your child see herself as a capable, likable human being, one of the best things you can do is to encourage her to try new things, whether it's putting together a puzzle or riding a bicycle. Such accomplishments will give her a sense of pride and self-confidence that no amount of external praise can duplicate.

Of course, you'll want to praise your child—and you should. Positive comments from parents help children feel good about themselves. But preschoolers are surprisingly sophisticated intellectually, so you need to be careful how you go about it. When your child is successful, praise her efforts rather than the outcome. Excessive praise, like "You're the best baseball player I've ever seen!" rings false, even to a big-headed four-year-old. Likewise, if you praise your child too frequently, it can begin to sound meaningless. Extreme praise also can cause children to feel pressure, because they feel they can't live up to your expectations. Comments like "You're the handsomest child in your class" or "You're absolutely brilliant" may lead your child to internalize unrealistic expectations—extreme good looks and true brilliance are rare commodities in the real world.

In fact, studies have found that praising a child's intelligence with comments like "You're so smart" can actually backfire, by making them less likely to try new things for fear of failing and losing their "smart" status. When children are praised for working hard and concentrating, on the other hand, it encourages them to sustain their motivation, performance, and self-esteem.

In all areas, try to make your praise contingent on what your preschooler actually does well. When she draws a picture, say something like, "I like how curly the little girl's hair is," rather than making a generic comment—"What a beautiful picture!" When your child is playing nicely with a sibling, tell her why she's doing such a good job: "You're really sharing nicely with your brother."

Another key to self-esteem is feeling like you make a difference in the world. By enlisting your child's help around the house, you'll tell her how important she is. Try saying things like, "It's really helpful to me when you put your clothes in the hamper at night," or "It's so nice when you hang up your wet towel. Having a big kid to help me sure makes my life easier!"

Children feel better about themselves when they feel in control of themselves, but they need firm limits in order to understand how to remain in control. It's the rare child who will curtail misbehavior without parental intervention. Don't be afraid to say no to your child's requests or to discipline her when the situation calls for it. Although some parents worry that discipline may damage their child's self-esteem, in fact, it does just the opposite. It teaches children how to behave, which makes them feel more confident and capable of moving successfully through life.

A final component of self-esteem is offering your child unconditional love. Give her unsolicited hugs and kisses, tell her how much you love her, and spend time doing mutually enjoyable activities together. Create an environment in which your child feels safe being who she is, even if she's not on her best behavior. Discipline your child when she requires it, but let her know it's her *behavior* you don't like—you'll always love *her* no matter what.

Fostering resilience

People who can bounce back from failure are often the most successful in the long run. Help your child become more resilient by teaching her to keep setbacks in perspective and by helping her set realistic expectations for herself. It's the rare child who jumps on a two-wheeled bike and begins riding quickly and easily or who learns to count without so much as a single stumble. Let her know that everyone struggles when they're learning new things, give her lots of encouragement, and stay close by so you can see when she's getting frustrated and it's time to put the new task aside.

If she gets down in the dumps because her friends are better at things than she is, encourage her to focus on self-improvement rather than keeping pace with her peers. Point out that some children are good at art or soccer, others are good at remembering songs or climbing on the monkey bars, but no one is good at everything. Let her know that she can improve at almost anything with practice, then highlight her strengths by saying, "Lisa may be able to throw the ball farther than you, but you really understand the rules of the game," or "Jason draws very well, but you are very patient and careful when you're coloring."

By helping your child learn to accept her shortcomings while valuing her strengths, she'll be able to rebound in tough times and learn to seek out opportunities in which she knows she can do well.

Trucks and tea sets

Your three- to four-year-old's gender identity

Maybe you found out what sex your baby was when it was still in your womb, or perhaps you waited for the moment when you gave birth and heard, "It's a girl!" or "It's a boy!" Either way, you undoubtedly reveled in discovering the gender of your child, because that piece of information gave you a clue as to who your offspring was (and would become) as a person.

There are still many unknowns about how children come to exhibit the personality differences that identify them as male or female. And the subject is quite hotly debated—some people believe hormones dictate identity while others argue that the environment is the cause of gender variations. In all likelihood, both factors play a critical role in creating masculinity and femininity.

One of the most important things to keep in mind when thinking about the sex of your child is that there are more differences among children of the same sex than there are between the sexes. In other words, two little girls may be much less similar than another little girl and little boy. In addition, there is a wide range of "normal" male and female behavior, so you shouldn't worry if your son or daughter doesn't conform to precise descriptions of typical behavior. That said, many experts now believe that there are certain inborn traits that distinguish males from females.

Your child's gender identity, or how he views himself, begins forming very early. Sex hormones create certain biological differences in the way boys' and girls' brains are organized even before they are born. As infants, girls tend to be more sensitive to voices; they usually begin talking earlier than boys and remain more verbal throughout their lives. They also are better able to read other people's facial expressions, and they pick up subtle information—like body language—from the environment more easily than boys.

Boys, on the other hand, tend to be more adept at things like understanding physical relationships—where one object is in relation to another or moving a three-dimensional object around in their minds. They also are more likely to be aggressive and to gravitate toward more physical activities.

Once out in the world, a baby also comes under environmental influences. Despite your best intentions to create a gender-neutral setting, your child probably has picked up subtle clues about what it means to be a boy or girl from you. Everything from the way you cuddled him and played with him as a baby (parents, especially fathers, typically engage in more motor activity with boys while they offer more interpersonal stimulation to girls) to strangers' well-intentioned comments like "She's so pretty" or "He's so strong" can give him a sense of "appropriate" behavior.

Like most everything in the realm of child development, children go through typical stages in acquiring a gender identity. During the preschool years, children tend to embark on a period of heavy-duty gender identification that includes not only an awareness of the physical differences between boys and girls but also an insistence on adopting somewhat rigid behaviors and attitudes based on how they believe men and women behave. They also may "fall in love with" the opposite-sex parent and go through a period of wanting to explore other children's bodies for clues about what distinguishes boys from girls.

DEVELOPMENTAL MILESTONE
Distinguishing gendered behavior

Put a group of preschoolers in a room, and the girls will probably gather together in a quiet corner, sharing ideas on how to play a game of house or dress-up, while the boys will drift off to the cars or blocks, which they'll eventually start smashing together in ever louder and more raucous play scenarios. It sounds like an exaggeration, but most parents and teachers of young children can attest to the fact that three- and four-year-olds have clearly assimilated many of society's most deeply ingrained ideas about gender behavior.

Study after study of young children has found that, in general, boys prefer gross motor activity—running, climbing, tumbling, kicking, jumping—while girls spend more time with dolls and other quieter play activities. That doesn't mean that young children won't be able to play nicely with their opposite-sex peers. In fact, boys and girls often will play a game of house or dress-up together, and during the early preschool years, boys are likely to experiment with female roles by dressing up in high heels and earrings (much to their fathers' chagrin). If you're worried about this early cross-dressing, it can help to remind yourself that your child's sexual orientation is dictated long before preschool, and any role-playing during childhood has less to do with sex than with a curiosity about outward appearances.

Gender roles tend to become more distinct as the preschool period progresses, with boys saying things like "Dolls are for girls," even if they've never heard such comments at home, and girls insisting on wearing dresses and wanting to play with their mothers' makeup. No one knows for certain why this happens, but it's probably the result of children's fragile self-images. Because their self-concepts are so newly formed, they feel the need to exaggerate their identities in order to make them seem more deeply ingrained.

In addition, young children tend to think in fairly concrete terms. To their way of thinking, a boy is a boy because he is big and strong, while a girl is a girl because she wears dresses and jewelry. They've identified the most obvious manifestations of male and female, but they lack the intellectual sophistication to understand the less superficial similarities and differences among people.

When you understand their logic, you can see that there's no reason to panic about your young child's choices or to make him feel guilty about wanting to be boyish. Eventually, he'll probably seem somewhat more relaxed about the whole gender issue (although even school-age children don't mingle much with the opposite sex until adolescence). If you want to broaden your preschooler's experience, you can encourage your son to do more traditionally female activities and vice versa. If you participate, he'll most likely be interested in just about anything you suggest.

Identifying with same-sex parent

Because of their fascination with male and female roles, preschoolers increasingly look to their same-sex parents for guidance about how to behave. You've been one all along, but your status as your child's role model will become even more important as he heads into these highly impressionable years.

Now is a good time to start thinking about what kind of message you want to send your child about men and women. Do you want to reinforce traditional sex roles? Or would you rather have your children see something different from what you likely grew up with?

Studies have shown that children whose mothers work outside the home have broader views about sex roles than those who have stay-at-home moms. But that doesn't mean that a mother who stays at home is dooming her child to a narrow concept of women's capabilities. If Mom makes a conscious effort to present a more open-minded interpretation of the female role in the family—by playing ball with the children and doing yardwork and traditional handyman projects alongside Dad—she can convey the message that women are capable of taking on all sorts of tasks. Likewise, if fathers participate in childcare, cooking, and cleaning, children will see that both men and women have a wide range of possible skills and responsibilities.

Becoming fascinated by bodies

Along with the advent of masculine and feminine behavior comes an increased interest in the physical differences between males and females. While toddlers will note that a boy has a penis and a girl has a vagina, preschoolers may want to see and touch other children's (or even parents') genitals.

Nudity. Some parents aren't comfortable being naked in front of their children—even as babies. Others feel it's important to send a message to children that nude bodies are healthy and normal and nothing to be ashamed of. Even if you fall into the latter camp, however, household nudity can get tricky just now, when you can feel your child's curious eyes examining your body the second you remove your clothing.

There are no strict rules for how to handle your child's burgeoning interest in your body. Probably the best advice is this: As long as both you and your child are comfortable, you can continue to undress in front of him. But if you start feeling awkward with his prying eyes, or if he starts becoming overly giddy or giggly, it's better to impose a few privacy rules. (Children can usually sense their parents' discomfort, so even if your child doesn't seem to feel awkward, let your own feelings about the matter carry equal weight.) When you start to get undressed, say, "I'm going to close the door now so I can change my clothes in private. Then I'll come out, and we can read a book."

Likewise, it's probably a good idea to draw the line when your child wants to touch your body. A casual caress here and there is no big deal, but some children actually grab their father's penises or pinch their mother's nipples. If your child ventures into that kind of territory, you should let him know that your body is private and you'd prefer that he not touch it. This approach serves a dual purpose: It lets him know that he isn't allowed to touch other people with complete abandon, and it can communicate the important message that it's not okay for him to let other people touch his private parts.

Playing doctor. If young children are curious about their parents' bodies, they're likely to be even more so about those of their peers, whose bodies also happen to be much more accessible. Some preschoolers never experiment physically with their playmates. But the majority, if given the opportunity, will want to "play doctor" with playmates or with their own siblings.

Happening upon your child in a state of undress with another child—especially if the other child is of the opposite sex—can be an unnerving experience for even the most laid-back parent. But your response can send a strong message to your child about his sexuality—acting shocked or disgusted can make him feel dirty or ashamed—so it's important for you to prepare yourself for this possibility and formulate a response ahead of time.

Probably the best response is to remain casual but to redirect the children's activity to something else. You can simply say, "You two need to put your clothes on. Then let's go play in the sandbox." Later, when you're alone with your child, tell him that it's natural to be curious about how other people's bodies look, but it's better to ask you about it than to touch another child. You also can get a book with drawings that will let him examine pictures of real bodies up close. Then, if you don't want it to happen again, stay nearby to loosely supervise your child's playdates, and set some basic rules for playing with other children: Clothes on, doors open.

If the activity included a child from another family, it's a good idea to let the other parents know what happened. Put yourself in their position: Wouldn't you want to know what your child is up to on a playdate? If you think about it like that, you can see why it's a good idea to force yourself to make the call, even if you dread it. Don't blame the other parents or the other child, and don't allow them to blame you or your child. Childhood sexual exploration is almost always consensual, and it's really a moot point which child started it.

Most often, such sexual exploration is harmless—evidence more of preschoolers' natural curiosity than any real sexual interest, although the touching that occurs may feel quite good to your child. But there are certain types of play that are more dangerous and should be curtailed firmly and immediately: If your child is with another child who is several years older, if he seems frightened or angry (rather than cheerful and giggly), or if the activity involves more than looking or simple touching (if there is oral contact with the genitals, penetration with fingers or other objects, or anal or vaginal intercourse) you should alert the other parents and seek the advice of your pediatrician, who can help you determine if your child has been abused and needs further counseling.

Dealing with masturbation. To refer to the touching that typically goes on in the preschool set as "masturbation" is actually overdramatizing the issue. Although young children often touch and fondle their genitals, they aren't masturbating in the adult sense. Since they aren't burdened with adult notions of what's sexually appropriate, they're simply touching a part of their bodies in a way that feels good. But they're not trying to achieve orgasm or consciously give themselves sexual pleasure. At this age, genital touching is used more as a way to relax and stave off anxiety, or simply out of unconscious habit.

Even so, since our society doesn't condone public fondling, it's a good idea to let your child know that he needs to limit his activity. When you see your child touching himself, say, "I know it feels good to touch yourself, but that's something you do in private, like going to the bathroom." Don't expect him to get the message immediately. Just like learning to pick up his toys or put his clothes away, this is a lesson that will take time to learn. But if you are consistent, gentle, and nonjudgmental in your message, he'll learn to save his genital touching for when he's alone, without being saddled with lifelong guilt about it.

Naming body parts. As curious as your child is about his anatomy, he most likely knows the names of all his body parts. But if he doesn't, now is definitely the time to teach him. It's best to use the correct anatomical names: penis, scrotum, vulva, vagina. They might not trip off the tongue as easily as euphemisms, but they'll give your child the (correct) impression that the penis or vulva is as normal as, say, a nose or knee. Shrouding them in euphemisms, on the other hand, can make them seem bad, embarrassing, or dirty.

Look for opportunities to talk about bodies as those chances come up naturally during the course of your day. Bathtime is an obvious option, getting dressed for bed is another one. Try to offer information in a calm, matter-of-fact way, just as you would if you were talking about an ear or an eyelid. If you're bashful or uneasy, your child will sense your discomfort and may come to believe there's something wrong with him, or at least with those parts of him.

CONFLICT
Rigid versus flexible sex roles

Although preschoolers have a sense of what it means to be a boy or girl in our culture, their ideas are far from complex or complete, nor are they very solid. In fact, it might be surprising to know that your child, even as he insists on being boyish, may believe that he can someday become a mommy, even after you explain that only women can have babies. Likewise a little girl might actually believe that it would be possible for her to become a boy if, for instance, she wore a baseball cap to bed every night or engaged in some other magical activity.

The possibility of becoming the opposite sex may be, in part, what causes children to divide into two gender-based camps at this age. Perhaps they're worried that by playing with children of the opposite sex they will actually turn into that sex.

In any case, the seeming impermanence of gender identity at this age might cause your child some anxiety. Think about it: The idea that you might wake up one morning as someone else would be disconcerting, to say the least! Little boys might worry that there's something wrong with them if they feel the urge to play with dolls, particularly if they're getting the message at home that dolls are for girls. Likewise, some little girls might long to ham it up with the boys who are playing cowboys, even as their girlfriends play in the dress-up corner. If for no other reason than that, it's a good idea to encourage your child to take the broadest view of gender he can, by providing him with plenty of different toys, playmates, and play experiences. Letting your child know it's okay to experiment with other roles can give him the message that he's okay just the way he is.

Another source of gender anxiety is children's bodies. Since penises are the most visible manifestation of gender at this age, much of preschoolers' concern centers around this appendage. For instance, boys may worry that they will lose their penises, a situation that can cause them to constantly touch their genitals. Girls may be troubled about the fact that they don't have a penis like their father and yet they don't look like their mother, who has pubic hair and big breasts, either.

It's important to reassure young children that their bodies are normal and healthy just the way they are, and to let them know that, although they will grow and change, they will always be a boy or a girl—even though they might not actually believe in the permanence of gender until age five or six.

How it feels to be me

The male perspective ...

I love being a boy! That means I'm big and strong. When my dad is at home, I follow him around and help him with things, because we're the men of the house. We do things like take out the recycling (I can carry the empty milk cartons) and fix the leaky faucet. I hold the tools while Dad hammers. When I get to school, I just like to play with the boys. My friend Jake says girls are boring, and I think he's right. They don't like to get dirty like we do, and they don't yell as loud.

The female perspective ...

I love being a girl! My mommy told me there are special things that only girls can do, like have babies and feed babies with their breasts. Even if my brother wanted to, he couldn't do that! I like to watch my mommy when she gets ready for work in the morning. She takes a shower, puts on lotion, then dries her hair and puts on her makeup. Sometimes she lets me put on a little, too, and it makes me feel so grown up. When I get together with my friends, I like to do what my mommy does when she has friends over: sit and talk. We pretend to make tea and let our babies play on the floor. It's fun to act like an adult!

YOU AND YOUR CHILD
Handling your child's crush

Preschoolers emulate their same-sex parents. Boys look to their fathers for advice on how to be men, and girls look to their mothers to learn how to be women. But both boys and girls go through a stage where they act like they've fallen in love with the opposite-sex parent. Sometimes it comes out in subtle ways—an adoring look now and then, or a desire to sit next to you at the dinner table. Other times, it's much more obvious. Your son may say, "Mommy, I want to marry you when I grow up," or your daughter may get jealous every time you and your spouse have a conversation (much less hug or kiss!).

First, it's important to know that such behavior is normal. Freud called this the Oedipal stage, when little boys want to kill their fathers and marry their mothers and little girls want to do the opposite (the Electra complex). Most experts today don't believe it's that extreme, but they say that the majority of preschoolers experience some version of a parental crush. Chalk it up to their confusion over types of love. Young children love their parents intensely, and they don't yet understand how to express that. They see you and your spouse and people on television acting romantically toward one another, and they simply imitate their role models.

Although you will need to let your child know that you won't be able to marry him, you'll also need to keep his feelings foremost in your mind. Don't laugh or tease him. He is very earnest about his affection for you, and you need to treat it respectfully. Let him know that you love him very much, and that you'll always be his mother no matter what. Then say, "But I'm married to Daddy. Someday, you'll fall in love and marry someone, too."

Listen to your child carefully during these discussions to be sure you understand any concerns he may have over your response. Some children may become anxious when they hear they are going to marry someone else. They can't imagine loving someone else, and they fear losing you. Reassure your child that the two of you will live together until he's a very big person and no longer needs you every day, but you'll always be there for him when he does need you—even after he has grown up.

If your child gets jealous when you and your spouse talk, hug, or kiss, set gentle limits. Say, "Mommy and Daddy need to show each other how much we love each other, but we'd like to include you, too. Would you like a family hug?" By the time your child is five or six, he'll be through this stage and into identifying with his same-sex parent. Why not enjoy the extra adoration while it lasts?

If your child...	Do say	Don't say
says "Look! My penis is big!"	"Yes, it is. That happens to all boys. Sometimes penises are small and soft, sometimes they get big and hard."	"Honey, I don't particularly want to look at your penis."
tells you it feels good to rub her pillow between her legs	"I'm sure. It's fine to do that as long as you do it in private."	"Nice girls don't do that. Please stop."
asks where babies come from	"They grow in a part of a woman's body called a uterus—right below the stomach."	"A stork brings them."
asks how babies get in the uterus	"Inside women's bodies are teeny tiny eggs and inside men's bodies are tiny things called sperm. Babies start to grow when the egg and sperm join together."	"You're too young to understand."
asks how the egg and sperm get together	"Sometimes grown-ups who love each other want to make a baby, so they put the man's penis in the woman's vagina. The sperm comes out of the penis and goes into the woman. Sometimes it finds an egg to join up with and starts a baby."	Don't launch into an explicit discussion of intercourse.

Answering questions about sex

You teach your child about plants, bugs, baseball, and language, and you have to teach him about sex, too. Right about now, your child is going to start becoming curious about things like where babies come from. Even if you feel squeamish about the topic, it's best for you to tackle it, rather than allowing your child to get lots of inaccurate information from peers or giving him the impression that the subject is naughty or embarrassing.

The first thing you should know is that sex education isn't a one-shot deal. It's a lifelong learning process. Most preschoolers aren't ready for, nor are they probably interested in, hearing a detailed description of intercourse. The information you give your child now needs to be geared to his stage of development and interest level. As he gets older, you need to continue looking for and responding to opportunities to talk about sexuality. Then, by the time he's an adult, he should have a healthy respect for and understanding of what it means to be a sexual being.

When your child asks you questions relating to sex, do your best to maintain a calm, matter-of-fact attitude. Let him know that his question is interesting and that he is welcome to ask you questions about the topic anytime.

HELPING YOUR CHILD GROW
Giving your child a broad sense of self

Boys and girls will never be exactly the same, nor would most of us like them to be. By the same token, most parents would like to raise both boys and girls who are strong *and* sensitive, rather than one or the other. Despite most preschoolers' rather narrow view of gender, it is possible to begin to instill in your child a more inclusive attitude toward masculinity and femininity.

Discourage gender discrimination. Your child may look disparagingly on a girlfriend who likes to dig in the dirt or a boy who plays with dolls. When you hear him or other children comment on it, set the record straight. You could say, "Actually, it's great for girls to play on the ground and get dirty. That can be a lot of fun for anyone." Or, "It's nice for boys to play with dolls, too. Then they'll grow up to be good daddies."

If your child suddenly shuns friends of the opposite sex, encourage him to reconnect with them. Ask why he doesn't want to play with Tracy or Kate anymore. If he says they just sit and have tea parties when they play, suggest that you have a playdate at the museum or zoo, where there is a different focus of activity. He'll see that he actually still has a lot in common with his female friends and that girls can be just as much fun as boys.

Be a non-gender-biased parent. Many studies have found differences in the way parents raise boys and girls. Parents tend to both praise and criticize their sons more than their daughters, they give sons more freedom at an earlier age, and they have been found to expect more from their sons on certain developmental tasks. But when parents expect more from their daughters, girls tend to live up to the task.

It may not be possible to completely eradicate your innate tendencies in dealing with boys and girls, but you can try. Look at everyday decisions and ask yourself: Would I do it differently if he was a girl, or if she was a boy?

Provide toys and activities that break down gender barriers. Give your son a doll and show him how much fun it can be to cuddle with it. Or give your daughter some trucks and take them to the sandbox. Likewise, you can enroll your son in dance lessons or your daughter in karate. The more experiences a child has with things outside his stereotypical realm, the more it will open his mind to unexpected possibilities.

Be a role model for both sons and daughters. It's important for mothers to teach their daughters how to be girls and for fathers to teach their sons how to be boys, but the reverse is true, too.

Mothers can teach boys how to be more at ease with things that are traditionally feminine, like being a good communicator, picking up on other people's feelings, and nurturing small creatures. Likewise, fathers can teach girls how to be more stereotypically masculine, by showing them how to do things like throw a softball or kick a soccer ball, or dig a hole.

Talk to your child about what he sees on television and in the world at large. Even now, TV often portrays men and women stereotypically—particularly in commercials, which are geared to sell products to a specific demographic market. If you see obvious examples of gender-typing, talk about it with your child. When a woman holds up a container of laundry detergent as if she couldn't live without it, you might say, "Many commercials just show mothers doing the wash, but Mommy and Daddy take turns doing it in our house, right?"

Whenever you see positive gender-role models, whether they're characters on a sitcom or people in the community—a woman construction worker or a man pushing a stroller—point them out to your child. He'll gradually get the sense that his options are unlimited.

Books about sex and reproduction

For parents:
- *From Diapers to Dating: A Parent's Guide to Raising Sexually Healthy Children* by Debra W. Haffner (Newmarket Press)

For children:
- *Did the Sun Shine Before You Were Born?* by Sol and Judith Gordon (Prometheus Books)
- *How You Were Born* by Joanna Cole (Mulberry)
- *What's the Big Secret?* by Laurie Krasny Brown and Marc Brown (Little Brown)

But I don't want to!

Your three- to four-year-old's behavior

When your child was a baby, taking care of her was easy. You fed her, diapered her, bathed her, played simple games with her. Although she was needy and sometimes demanding, she didn't misbehave. Then she turned two, and you got a dose of reality: Children can be a handful. Two-year-olds are notoriously mischievous. They love to do things like throw your glasses in the toilet, draw on the wall with crayons, and toss peas on the floor to see how far they'll roll. Even so, there's a certain innocence in toddlers' antics. At that age, your child often didn't understand that she was doing anything wrong, and, even if she did break a known rule, you cut her lots of slack: "She's only two," you'd tell yourself.

By the time your child is a preschooler, however, she's starting to learn the rules. You may feel like you've repeated certain cardinal rules—"No hitting! Use your words"—hundreds of times, and you probably have. Likewise, your child has been reprimanded for dozens of other specific incidents, and she's seen other children get scolded, so she understands much of what's considered out-of-bounds behavior. In fact, most preschoolers, especially older ones, have a healthy respect for rules and will recite them any chance they get. You'd think, then, that your child would actually start following them. Unfortunately, that's not the way it is.

Misbehavior is more difficult to understand at this age, because there is a willful component to it. "But she *knows* better," you may groan to yourself, when you see her hitting a friend on a playdate or swiping a toy from her younger brother. For that reason and others, your tolerance may be stretched to its limit on more than a few occasions over the next couple of years. But if you understand what's behind this near-universal refusal to play by the book, and respond to her behavior calmly and consistently (that's the hard part), you'll be better able to handle her ups and downs. Along the way, keep this light-at-the-end-of-the-tunnel thought in mind: By the time they're five, most children enter a fairly well behaved stage.

DEVELOPMENTAL MILESTONE
Becoming more headstrong

You've decided that every Thursday afternoon, you'll leave your youngest child with a baby-sitter so that you and your preschooler can spend a few hours alone together. Every Thursday afternoon, you indulge in a fantasy: You envision the two of you playing happily at the park or giggling through a movie or sharing an ice-cream sundae. And every Thursday you are confronted by a brutal reality: Your child insists on climbing the park fence, then gets scratched and cries inconsolably; she doesn't want to see the movie that's playing; or she decides it's more fun to dribble ice cream onto the table than to scoop it into her mouth. "Why is she like this?" you may ask yourself, exasperated.

There's a good reason for her behavior, and it comes with the territory just now. Although two-year-olds have a "terrible" reputation, it's actually preschoolers who terrorize their parents, for one simple reason: They can. The central struggle for children this age is the need to carve out more independence and to gain more control over their lives. Because you're constantly clamoring for good behavior, your child feels that, in order to assert her autonomy, she must (almost by necessity) do the opposite. (It's not unusual for the primary caregiver to bear the brunt of her child's bad behavior. She spends more time with her child than her spouse, and, as a result, she also ends up serving as the most frequent naysayer.) It's actually a normal—crucial, even—aspect of your child's development.

Children this age can find many ways to be disobedient. But there are a few behaviors that are characteristic of preschoolers in particular. So, next time you worry that your child is the only one acting up while children in other homes are sitting calmly and reading, or saying please and thank you to their parents, remind yourself of this list—and the fact that nearly every young child (even that angelic neighbor) has pulled a number of these tricks at least once.

Whining. "But I don't want to go the store!" It's a simple statement. But when it's repeated dozens of times in the voice that many preschoolers adopt for their most adamant refusals—low, nasal, and peevish, interspersed with sniffles and moans—it can drive you up the wall. Why do children this age suddenly adopt this complaining tone? Usually, it's because they've tried different ways of expressing themselves, and they've discovered that this particular approach really gets your attention—and often works! Stifle whines before they wear down your resistance by saying, "No whining! If you want to whine, go to your room. But I'd be happy to listen to what you have to say if you say it in your nice voice."

If you know you're going to have to deny your child's request—which will probably bring on another bout of whining—try to distract her before she gets her whine machine fully revved up. "I was just about to make some cookies. Would you like to be my special helper?" Sometimes, the lure of a fun project or an interesting object—a bug on the windowsill, a picture of a lion in a magazine—will divert your child's mind from the subject at hand.

It also can be helpful to demonstrate for your child how annoying whining sounds. When your child is in a happy mood, say something in a whiny voice, then repeat it in a regular tone. Then ask your child, "Can you see why whining hurts my ears? Isn't it nicer to listen to a pleasant voice?" Although it might be tempting to give her a demonstration of whining when she's in a whiny mood, don't. It would sound like you were mocking her and hurt her feelings—both of which would only serve to blur the real issue.

Cursing. Young children emulate everything you say. When your child says, "Oh my goodness! I left my gloves at school!" you may smile at how adult she sounds. But if she says, "Sh——! I left my gloves at school!"—a situation that is just as likely to occur—you'll undoubtedly quake in horror. You may even be concerned that she's headed for a life of hooliganism. Don't worry. To preschoolers, there's no such thing as a bad word. Words are simply, well, words, and she believes that they're all created equally, especially if she hears you using them. That's why the first step toward extinguishing trash talk is cleaning up your own language. Children repeat what they hear, and it's unfair to expect them not to.

If you want to suppress your child's urge to utter obscenities, don't overreact. If she thinks she can get a rise out of you just by saying one word, you can bet you'll hear it again and again. Simply explain to her that some words are not nice to use because they make people upset and angry, and give her alternative words to use instead—*shoot, darn it, gosh, heck.* If she slips occasionally, don't make a big deal of it—even if she embarrasses you in public. Just remind her of the rule and move on. Anyone with preschoolers will understand your situation and won't look askance at your tactics.

Name-calling and taunting. Preschoolers have clued into the power of words, and they will begin to use them in hurtful ways, calling a friend "stupid" or saying to a sibling in a singsong voice, "You can't come with me, nah, nah, nah, nah, nah." Part of the problem is that your child is still short on empathy. But it's important to help her understand that, despite what it says in the popular "Sticks and stones may break my bones" rhyme, words *can* hurt a child's feelings.

Ask her how she would feel if someone called her stupid. Then say, "We don't talk to our friends like that. Can you think of some way to make your friend feel better?" Try to get her to apologize—whether it's with words or a hug or kiss—but it's more effective if the idea comes from her. To keep put-downs out of your child's repertoire, be a good example. Watch what you say, and, if you hear a character in a cartoon saying something mean, use it as a teaching opportunity. Point out the indiscretion to your child and remind her, "That's not a nice thing to say because it can hurt someone's feelings."

Talking back. When you ask your child to put on her clothes, she says, "No! I want to wear pajamas to school." When you tell her it's time to brush her teeth, she says, "I don't have to. You can't make me." When you warn her that she'll have to say good-bye to her friend in five minutes, she says, "No, *ten* minutes." During the preschool years, it's not uncommon for the simplest tasks to become enormous battles not only because your child often refuses to cooperate, but also because of the *manner* in which she refuses to cooperate. It's completely maddening to have a pint-size person who still relies on you for almost everything using a disrespectful tone of voice! But there's a reason she's being snotty: She's trying to assert her independence and wield her newfound power.

You don't have to put up with rude behavior, however. You can say, "I understand that you don't want get dressed now, but I don't like your tone of voice." Then, explain why you expect her to do as you've asked: "You must put on your clothes, because children aren't allowed to wear pajamas to preschool." With a reason for the request, she may find it easier to acquiesce. If your child continues her sassiness, give her a time-out (one minute for each year of her age) and say, "You need to be alone until you can speak politely."

Sneaking. You tell your child she can't have a cookie until after dinner. Then, five minutes later, you find crumbs on the counter (and a guilty look on her face). Willful misbehavior often crops up at this age, because of preschoolers' push for more independence. They'll do things that test your rules—and your patience. Eliminate sneaky behavior by providing a natural consequence for your child's actions. The cookie thief can't have a cookie after dinner if she sneaks one beforehand. Remain firm. If you give in, you'll only reinforce the behavior. It's critical that you let her know she'll be penalized if she doesn't follow the rules.

CONFLICT
Wanting your approval versus testing your limits
Preschoolers adore their parents and want nothing more than to make them proud. Want proof? Just look at your child's face the next time she shows you a picture she drew or demonstrates her newfound ability to swing from the parallel bars at the playground. Her look of eager anticipation will show you how much she craves your affection, attention, and approval.

And yet she's capable of deliberate disobedience, of doing things that she knows will invoke your ire and disapproval. Why? In all likelihood, she can't help herself. Preschoolers' self-control is still shaky at best. (She knows she shouldn't take a toy away from her friend, but she really wants to play with that toy, and she wants to play with it *now*.) Pair that with her developmental urge to stake out her own rights and assert her need for greater freedom, and you have a situation that's ripe for misbehavior.

Even so, misbehaving actually makes your child feel quite anxious, because she worries that by breaking a rule she's risking losing your love. It's important to let her know that you'll always love her, no matter what she does. And it's okay to let her win some battles. If she wants to wear the pink shirt instead of the blue one you chose, or eat peanut butter and jelly instead of tuna fish, you're not being overly permissive by giving in to her demand. Being allowed to make some choices and take charge of her own destiny in small ways makes her feel good about herself and gives her the self-confidence to progress to the next step in her development.

But children this age also crave limits. Even as they push the envelope of your rules, they want you to show them where the boundaries are and to enforce them strictly and consistently. It sounds contradictory, but preschoolers are reassured by regular, predictable discipline. Without your limits, they feel wild and dangerously out of control. Just keep your child's internal struggle in mind when you discipline her. Remember that she fears losing your love by being "bad," and let her know that it's the behavior you don't like, not her.

YOU AND YOUR CHILD
Becoming a disciplinarian

It can be quite a shock for parents when their little angels first begin to misbehave. Most of us find it much easier to love and nurture our children than to say no and discipline them. But, as your child goes through the preschool stage, she needs you to tell her the rules, to remind her of the right way to do things, and to teach her how to have self-control, so that by the time she enters the school-age years she has internalized your message and actually has a solid base of self-control and a fairly good grasp of right and wrong.

That said, you're going to have some tough challenges ahead of you. For one thing, you may not ever have been in charge before, and the prospect can be quite scary. You may worry you'll sound like your own parents when you lay down the family rules, a prospect that can seem very unappealing. Or you may be concerned that your child will come to resent you if you're always the one who says no. Such fears are perfectly normal and nearly universal. But you'll have to overcome them if you want to be the kind of parent who can guide her child firmly and lovingly through this sometimes challenging stage. Here are some things you can do to bolster your inner disciplinarian:

Talk to other parents. Commiserating with people who are in the same position as you are can make you feel better, and you may get some tips on how to handle certain situations by asking other parents how they have handled them. Sometimes the best advice comes from people down in the trenches with you.

Read books. Some parents feel like they don't know how to discipline. Maybe they received very little structure as a child, or perhaps they were raised by very harsh disciplinarians. In either case, they didn't learn what it means to discipline effectively with love and respect. Fortunately, there are dozens of child-rearing books that address the subject of discipline, and most offer a number of specific examples for handling common misbehaviors. Gather ideas for how to deal with challenging behaviors from books, but don't be afraid to tweak them to fit your own particular child and situation.

Question your motivation. If you submit to your child's request (which is fine some of the time), make sure it's not because you simply want to avoid the difficult task of setting limits, but rather because you think it's an issue actually worth compromising on: She wants a cookie for an afternoon snack, say; it's not that she wants cookies (and nothing else) for dinner. If you can feel yourself reacting in ways that merely aim to maintain a happy atmosphere or to please your child, think twice before letting her have her way. Remember: She is relying on you to provide boundaries and teach her what's acceptable and what's not.

Some good child-rearing books

- *1-2-3 Magic: Effective Discipline for Children 2–12* by Thomas W. Phelan, Ph.D. (Child Management)
- *The Discipline Book: Everything You Need to Know to Have a Better-Behaved Child—From Birth to Age Ten* by William Sears, M.D., and Martha Sears, R.N. (Little Brown)
- *Don't Be Afraid to Discipline* by Dr. Ruth Peters (Golden Books)
- *Positive Discipline for Preschoolers: For Their Early Years—Raising Children Who Are Responsible, Respectful, and Resourceful* by Jane Nelsen, Roslyn Duffy, and Cheryl Erwin (Prima)
- *Raising Your Spirited Child: A Guide for Parents Whose Child Is More Intense, Sensitive, Persistent, and Energetic* by Mary Sheedy Kurcinka (Harper Perennial)
- *Time-In: When Time-Out Doesn't Work* by Jean Illsley Clark (Parenting Press)

Handling challenges to your authority

Once you get the hang of being in charge, you may find your child's misbehavior even more intolerable. In certain egregious situations, like when she turns over the toy box you just finished filling or she blows bubbles in her milk immediately after you've told her not to, you may even think to yourself, "How dare she defy me?" Indeed, it can be difficult to cope with the fact that, despite your best efforts to set reasonable, clear rules, your child still disobeys. You may wonder what's wrong with your parenting style and be concerned that perhaps she's just a "bad seed."

At moments like this it can help to remember that her behavior is part of a developmental process. Children don't learn something after hearing it once, just like you didn't pick up algebra after one day of class. They need to hear rules over and over again before they actually sink in. Likewise, children need to test the rules to make sure they're really set in stone. You may have said yesterday that it's not okay to run with a lollipop in your mouth, but your child may do it dozens more times just to see if the rule stays the same. (That's one of the reasons it's important to set rules and stick with them.) Just continue doggedly repeating the rules. Eventually she'll catch on—and you'll be rewarded with a well-behaved child.

Managing your anger

Some days you can face your child's defiance with an equanimity that would make the Dalai Lama proud. Other days, you're not quite as in control. If you're tired, stressed out, or just having a bad day, your child's misbehavior can be like a match igniting your very short fuse. Controlling your own temper can be as difficult as setting limits for your child. Here are some helpful tactics for keeping your composure.

Think like a three-year-old. Often, what's most galling about children's misbehavior is the fact that it seems so intentional. If you feel like your child is out to get you, take a step back and review her behavior from *her* perspective. You'll undoubtedly see that she is angry or upset about something else and her lashing out isn't directed at you so much as at the world. Seeing things from her point of view will help you step back from the precipice of your own anger and respond to her with more love and compassion.

Breathe before you speak. There are times you'll feel the urge to say something mean to your child—"You're acting like a spoiled brat!"—because you feel pushed to the brink. When you feel a mean-spirited comment forming, take a few deep breaths and rephrase your statement: "I know you want a new toy, but we're here to buy diapers. We can't buy a new toy every time we go to the store." If you do say something nasty to your child, be sure to apologize later. Let her know that you were angry and tired and that you're sorry for what you said, which will serve two purposes: First, it will make amends to your child. Second, it will teach her that even adults say "I'm sorry" when they do something wrong.

How it feels to be me

Some days it's easy to be good. I feel happy and content just being with you and doing fun things. Other days, I can't help doing naughty things. Like one day, my little brother took the toy car I'd been playing with. It made me so mad that I hit him before I even thought about it. When he started crying, I knew I was going to get in trouble. And I felt bad when I saw the red spot I made on his forehead. But I didn't think about that before I hit him. I just knew I wanted to hurt him because he hurt me. I wanted to play with that car!

I get a little scared of myself sometimes, like when I get really out of control. I get so mad I'll run around the room like crazy or yell really loud. Then, I need you to help me get under control. When I see that you're still calm (and that you still love me), it helps me start to calm down, too, and makes me feel safe again.

Stay emotionally detached. This is harder than it sounds, but if you can watch your child act out without getting emotionally involved, you can suppress your anger. Try speaking in a calm, even, quiet tone. Most of us have the urge to yell when we're mad, but by speaking quietly, you can diffuse the intensity of your feelings so you can deal more effectively with your child's out-of-control emotions.

Walk away. Sometimes, you're too hot under the collar to cope. When you're feeling close to exploding, remove yourself from the situation before you say or do something you'll regret later. Say to your child, "I'm too angry to deal with you right now. I'm going to take a time-out." Then go to your room and shut your door for a few minutes. Lie down and take a few deep breaths or do some easy stretches. Putting some distance between yourself and the issue will help you regain the poise you need to deal with the situation and may even help your child see that she has pushed too far.

If your child...	Do	Don't
throws a temper tantrum in the supermarket	Ignore her or calmly remove her from the situation.	Buy into her drama by getting emotionally overwrought.
steals another child's toy	say, "That's Melissa's toy, and it upsets her when you take it. Remember how sad you were when Doug took your airplane?"	say, "You're being so mean. Give that toy back right now."
bangs loudly on the piano	say, "You feel like being noisy. Why don't you take this pot and spoon into the backyard and make some music out there?"	say, "You can't make that much noise. It's driving me crazy!"
uses a curse word	say, "That's not a nice word" (calmly), or just ignore it.	Wash her mouth out with soap.

HELPING YOUR CHILD GROW
Disciplining effectively

Many of us have a negative view of discipline because we equate the term with punishment, which is fraught with negative connotations. We imagine the harsh schoolmaster, the prison warden, the dispassionate judge. But, when it comes to child rearing, discipline more appropriately means "to teach." Discipline is a way of showing your child right from wrong, molding her behavior so she can get along in society and giving her a sense of external control so that eventually she will develop self-control. It's a way of providing limits for your child, who lacks a built-in system of behavioral checks and balances.

When you've said "No!" for the thousandth time, it may seem

that you have very few options when it comes to creating boundaries in your child's world. But the truth is, there actually are quite a few different techniques that have been shown to be effective in shaping children's behavior. Here are some of the best:

Offer choices. Because preschoolers crave independence, giving them options can make them feel like they have free reign in their universe. Take care to avoid overwhelming your child, however. Instead of saying, "What would you like to wear to preschool today?" give her a choice between two outfits. Though she may be unable to make up her mind when faced with a closetful of clothes, when given only two options, she feels she's in charge without being bewildered.

Set a good example. Since children imitate their parents' behavior, it's critical that you do as you would have your child do. Treat your child and other people respectfully, keep your temper under control, eliminate derogatory terms and obscenities from your vocabulary, and listen to other people's points of view. Your child will be more likely to follow your example than to heed your words.

Praise your child. One of the best ways to shape your child's conduct is to let her know when she does something right. Choose a behavior—straightening her room, for instance—and compliment her when she takes steps in the right direction. Make your praise specific. Rather than "You're such a good girl," say "Look at how well you picked up your toys. Good job!"

Anticipate and avoid problems. Before you're going to do something—whether it's to meet a friend for a playdate or to run errands—let your child know how you expect her to behave. Review some simple ground rules: You must share toys nicely, use your words when you want something, and take turns.

Likewise, give her plenty of warning when you're going to change activities. If it's nearing time to leave the playground, say,

"You can play for five more minutes, then we need to go home and fix dinner." Some children need more warning than others. Pay attention to your child's temperament. If she needs extra time to adjust to transitions, give her 10- or 15-minute warnings.

Some children are especially difficult to deal with at certain times of day. If your child seems to hit the wall every day about 4 P.M., for instance, don't plan big outings during that time. If the grocery store is a particularly difficult place for her to go (it is for lots of kids this age), bring along her favorite toy or allow her to pick out one treat if she behaves well.

Explain the reasons behind your rules. To an adult, it's obvious why you can't eat a box of animal crackers before dinner. But your child may not have any idea why you've said no to her request. If you tell her the reason—"We're going to eat dinner very soon, and if you eat too much now you won't be hungry for the meal I've made for you"—she's less likely to kick up a fuss.

Teach empathy. Understanding someone else's point of view doesn't come naturally to a preschooler. Your child needs your help to see that her actions upset or hurt someone else. If you repeatedly point out how her behavior effects others—"When you called Joni a baby it hurt her feelings,"—she'll begin to internalize the message. With preschoolers, you can also turn the tables and ask them how they'd feel in a certain situation—"How would it make you feel if Joni called you a baby?" Most children this age are emotionally sophisticated enough to be able to imagine a scenario, complete with emotional content.

Use logical consequences. When your child has done something wrong, one of the best ways to teach her not to repeat the misbehavior is to show her the consequences of her actions. (When she falls because she's not looking where she's going, the scrapes she gets on her knees are potent reminders of the rule "Always look where you're going.") If she draws on the wall, for instance, you could have her help you clean it off. Showing her how difficult it is to remove crayon from the wall will be more effective in teaching her not to do it again than giving her a time-out, which is unrelated to the misbehavior.

Employ strategic time-outs. If you give your child a time-out every time she misbehaves, the technique will lose its effectiveness. But if you utilize the strategy only in certain instances, like when your child's behavior is out of control, it can be a useful tool.

Teach your child to view time-outs not as a punishment so much as a break in the action, a time to reflect on the situation and get herself under control. Give your child one minute of time alone for every year of her age, and make sure to discuss the issue that caused the time-out with her at the end of the session. Say, "Do you understand why you needed to be alone?" Let her tell you in her own words what happened, so you're sure she gets it.

Create a reward chart. For a preschooler, a chart can be good motivator, because it provides an objective view of her progress. Charts are best reserved for especially hard-to-change behaviors, like sharing with a sibling. Design a days-of-the-week calendar, and let your child choose some stickers she likes. Then, at the end of each day, let her put a sticker up if she succeeded in getting along with her sibling. If she's having a bad day, warn her—"You won't be able to put a sticker on the chart today if you don't start sharing with your brother"—and follow through on your threats.

Engage her in problem solving. Since preschoolers love to feel like they're taking charge of their lives, one way to encourage good behavior is to ask them for suggestions for dealing with a particularly tough problem, like sibling fighting or sitting quietly in the grocery cart. Often, children will come up with remarkably effective strategies, like playing in separate parts of the room or taking books along to the grocery store.

Bedtime battles

Resisting bedtime is one of the classic problems of the preschool years. Nearly every child goes through a phase of dodging ("I'm just going to play this game one more time, then I'll go") and delaying ("Can I have one more kiss?") bedtime, or downright refusing to go to bed ("But I don't want to go to bed. I'm not even tired!"). But it's important for preschoolers to get between 10 and 12 hours of sleep per night, so you need to enforce strict bedtime rules. Here's how to make it easier:

- **Give her fair warning.** When bedtime is imminent, let your child know that it's time to start preparing. Say, "Five more minutes and then we're going to have our bath." Don't allow a lot of dillydallying.
- **Teach her to recognize bedtime on the clock.** If your child typically goes to sleep at 8 P.M., show her what that looks like on the kitchen clock. There's no arguing with something as objective as that!
- **Establish a pleasant bedtime routine.** Winding down at the end of the day is difficult for many preschoolers, but a calming routine helps them transition from day to night mode. For example, start with a warm bath. Then put on pajamas, brush teeth, and read a book or two. Keep your good-nights short but sweet—a warm hug and kiss, then "Sweet dreams" and leave the room.
- **Don't give into tricks.** If your child thinks she can push back her bedtime by asking you for more water or one more hug, she'll do it. Make it clear that she can have one glass of water, but no more. Then hang tough. Giving in sends the message that this strategy works.
- **Create a cozy, safe environment.** If your child is afraid of the dark, put a night-light in her room, leave the closet light on, allow her to go to sleep (if she can) with the overhead light on, or put the overhead light on a dimmer switch, and turn it down, but not off. Give her a soft toy or blanket to make her feel secure. Many preschoolers have given up such comfort objects during the day, but they may still need them at night. Don't let her go to bed with a menagerie of stuffed animals, though, or she'll play instead of sleep.
- **If she doesn't seem tired at bedtime, eliminate naps.** Children typically give up their naps sometime during the preschool years. If your child truly is not tired at bedtime (if she's not cranky and rubbing her eyes, she's probably not sleepy), eliminate her daytime nap and see if it becomes easier to get her to bed at night.

Teaching manners and morals

Preschoolers are not known for being particularly well-mannered. They have lots of energy—often too much for the situation at hand, like sitting quietly at the dinner table or listening while someone else speaks. Even so, you can begin to lay the ground rules and enforce some rudimentary manners in young children.

Make a plea for please and thank you. Get your child in the habit of asking for things by saying "please" and accepting things with a "thank you." Give her some time to get accustomed to using these words, and soon she should begin to understand that it's easier to get things she wants by asking nicely. Perhaps the best way to make these social niceties a normal part of your child's speech is to have her hear you using them regularly.

Practice being polite. When you're going to be in a situation in which you'll be meeting new people, rehearse polite behavior with your child. Show her how to shake hands, say hello, and make eye contact. Keep the atmosphere light and fun, and she'll enjoy these lessons in social etiquette.

Compliment polite behavior. Don't let good manners go unnoticed. Praise your child when you see her saying "Excuse me" or keeping quiet when she desperately wants to interrupt someone.

Set gentle limits on mealtime. Some preschoolers are almost physically incapable of sitting in their seats through an entire half-hour meal. To avoid mealtime battles, insist that your child sits while she eats, but don't expect her to sit through long family discussions. As for how she behaves during meals, try to build her repertoire of manners one skill at a time. If you're working on the rule "Don't speak with your mouth full," for instance, don't reprimand her for putting her elbows on the table. Save that for next month, when she'll have the first rule under her belt. Also, keep in mind that she'll enjoy family meals more and sit longer if she's included in the conversation. Ask her questions about her day and allow her to weigh in on things the adults are discussing. By keeping her involved, you'll see a big improvement in her ability to sit still.

Raising a moral child

During the early preschool years, most children have little understanding of morality because they are naturally egocentric. They think the world revolves around their needs and desires and haven't yet internalized the idea that other people have needs and wants, too. By the end of this stage, however, your child will begin to develop a conscience. She will see that her actions affect other people, and she'll know that she shouldn't lie, cheat, or steal (even though she may still not be able to control her impulses in this regard).

Because she's such a neophyte in the moral arena, long lectures about moral behavior will probably be lost on your child. Your best bet at this stage is to model morality. Let your child see you doing the right thing—returning extra change to the cashier, helping an elderly person across the street, carrying grocery bags for a pregnant neighbor—and she'll start to accept that this is the right way to behave. As you take moral actions, explain to your child why you're choosing to do so. Let her know that behaving conscientiously is not only good for other people, but it also makes you feel good inside.

Respect your child's uniqueness

All children learn to verbalize their emotions, socialize, and become more independent at their own unique pace. It's your job to support and encourage your child's natural schedule—and enjoy the adventure!

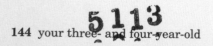